# Walking for Fitness

# Walking for Fitness
## FOURTH EDITION

### Lon H. Seiger
Texas A&M University–Corpus Christi

### James Hesson
Black Hills State University

Boston   Burr Ridge, IL   Dubuque, IA   Madison, WI   New York
San Francisco   St. Louis   Bangkok   Bogotá   Caracas   Kuala Lumpur
Lisbon   London   Madrid   Mexico City   Milan   Montreal   New Delhi
Santiago   Seoul   Singapore   Sydney   Taipei   Toronto

# McGraw-Hill Higher Education

*A Division of The **McGraw-Hill** Companies*

WALKING FOR FITNESS, WINNING EDGE SERIES
FOURTH EDITION

Published by McGraw-Hill, a business unit of The McGraw-Hill Companies, Inc., 1221 Avenue of the Americas, New York, NY 10020. Copyright © 2002, 1998, 1994 by The McGraw-Hill Companies, Inc. All rights reserved. No part of this publication may be reproduced or distributed in any form or by any means, or stored in a database or retrieval system, without the prior written consent of The McGraw-Hill Companies, Inc., including, but not limited to, in any network or other electronic storage or transmission, or broadcast for distance learning.

Some ancillaries, including electronic and print components, may not be available to customers outside the United States.

This book is printed on acid-free paper.

5 6 7 8 9 0 QPF/QPF 0 9 8 7 6 5 4

ISBN 0–07–235386–4

Vice president and editor-in-chief: *Thalia Dorwick*
Executive editor: *Vicki Malinee*
Developmental editor: *Carlotta Seely*
Senior marketing manager: *Pamela S. Cooper*
Project manager: *Richard H. Hecker*
Senior production supervisor: *Sandy Ludovissy*
Designer: *K. Wayne Harms*
Cover designer: *Lisa Gravunder*
Cover image: *Jim Cummins/FPG International*
Supplement producer: *Sandra M. Schnee*
Media technology producer: *Judi David*
Compositor: *Shepherd, Inc.*
Typeface: *10/12 Palatino*
Printer: *Quebecor World Fairfield, PA*

### Library of Congress Cataloging-in-Publication Data

Seiger, Lon H.
    Walking for fitness  /  Lon H. Seiger, James L. Hesson. — 4th ed.
        p.   cm. — (Winning edge series)
    Includes bibliographical references (p.   ) and index.
    ISBN 0-07-235386-4
    1. Physical fitness. 2. Walking. I. Hesson, James L. II. Title.
III. Winning edge series (Boston, Mass.)

GV502.S35   2002
613.7′176 — dc21                                          2001031260
                                                          CIP

The Internet addresses listed in the text were accurate at the time of publication. The inclusion of a website does not indicate an endorsement by the authors or McGraw-Hill, and McGraw-Hill does not guarantee the accuracy of the information presented at these sites.

www.mhhe.com

# PREFACE

*Walking for Fitness* is not intended to be a total fitness book. It focuses on the components of health-related fitness that are of greatest concern in our society—cardiovascular fitness and body composition. This book is designed to educate and motivate you to adopt fitness walking and other positive behaviors as part of an active, healthy lifestyle.

The message of this book is a powerful one. Each day of our lives we make choices—whether consciously or not—about our health. These choices have a cumulative effect, and over time they will either enhance or detract from our state of well-being. The challenge that *Walking for Fitness* poses is for you to choose fitness walking and healthy behaviors as a way of achieving optimal fitness and wellness throughout your lifetime.

Life is a journey, so enjoy it. Value your health by taking positive actions each day to make good health a part of your journey!

## AUDIENCE

This book is intended for walkers of any age, gender, background, and skill level. It has been developed to assist people to acquire the knowledge, attitudes, and skills necessary for participation in a lifelong fitness walking program. Although *Walking for Fitness* is designed primarily for an introductory course at the college level, it can also be used in a variety of other settings. The material is presented in a style that is easy for the beginning fitness walker to understand. Yet it offers the opportunity for more experienced walkers to achieve intermediate and advanced levels of knowledge and skill by thoroughly mastering the content.

## FEATURES

*Walking for Fitness* is a practical book, written in a style that is clear, concise, and inviting. Its content ranges from tips on what to wear while walking in different types of weather to applying the latest research on aerobic performance to your fitness walking program.

Many photographs complement the text, illustrating the how-to approach to proper walking technique. These photographs also provide motivational reinforcement to your fitness walking program. Various tables and boxes appear throughout the text to offer extra information to the interested reader.

In addition, this edition includes the following special features that enhance its use:

- Each chapter begins with a bulleted list of objectives and ends with a summary that reinforces the major points covered.

- Key terms are highlighted in boldface type in the text and are defined in complementary boxes.
- Fitness Tip boxes offer practical information related to walking, such as how to reduce the risk of dehydration, how to stay motivated, and how to set attainable goals.
- Assessments appear at the end of each chapter to assist you in developing and tracking your fitness walking program. These self-assessments can be used to determine your readiness for walking, improve your walking technique, and evaluate your level of wellness.
- The Rockport Fitness Walking Test is explained in detail, including how to take your pulse, determine your fitness category, and interpret the test results. The test is presented as an assessment in chapter 6.

## ANCILLARIES

To facilitate the use of *Walking for Fitness* in the classroom, a printed Test Bank is available to instructors. This ancillary features approximately 120 questions, including short-answer, true/false, and multiple-choice items.

## ACKNOWLEDGMENTS

We would like to thank the following reviewers, who provided us with expert commentary during the development of this text:

**Annemarie Boarman**
Kent State University

**June Decker**
Western New Mexico University

**Susan Hart**
New Mexico State University

**Nicole Lemon**
California State University-Fullerton

**Elaine McHugh**
Sonoma State University

We extend special appreciation to Dr. Larry Tentinger and Margie Hesson as contributing authors; to David Baker for his outstanding photography; to Jill Pankey and Lucia Vanderpool for their professional drawings; the models for their time and patience; and to Dr. David Leo, Dean Dee Hopkins, Dr. Sandra Harper, and Dr. Robert Furgason for their support.

Lon H. Seiger

James Hesson

# CONTENTS

Preface v

1    **The Walking Trend, 1**

2    **Benefits of Fitness Walking, 13**

3    **Clothing and Equipment, 29**

4    **Safety, 43**

5    **Warm-Up, Cool-Down, and Flexibility, 59**

6    **Fitness Walking Test, 71**

7    **Fitness Walking Programs, 85**

8    **Fitness Walking Techniques, 99**

9    **Strategies for Healthy Nutrition, 125**

10   **Healthy Weight and Body Fatness, 149**

11   **Sticking With It, 165**

12   **Wellness Through Healthy Lifestyles, 183**

**Appendix A    Walking-for-Fitness Exercise Log, 199**

**Appendix B    Resources for Fitness Walking, 201**

**References and Suggested Readings, 203**

**Index, 207**

# DEDICATION

To my wife Melissa and our three children, Von, Jensyn, and Keera; and to my mom and dad, sister Jodi, and brothers Radd and Darin—thanks for being "family."

Lon H. Seiger

To Margie, Jennifer, and David, for their support and love; and to all my students, who have taught me how to help them learn; and to the greatest teacher of all, who is with us every step of the way in our walk through life.

James L. Hesson

# THE **WALKING** TREND

## ▼ OBJECTIVES

*After reading this chapter, you should be able to do the following:*

* Understand the importance of walking in relation to *Healthy People 2010*.
* Describe the Surgeon General's Report on *Physical Activity and Health*.
* Define fitness walking.
* List several reasons why walking is the most popular physical activity.
* Explain why walking is an ideal form of physical activity.
* Discuss the relationship of walking to physical fitness.

## KEY TERMS

*While reading this chapter, you will become familiar with the following terms:*

► **Fitness Walking**

► **Healthy People 2010**

► **Life Expectancy**

► **Quality of Life**

► **Volksmarch**

► **Volksport**

*Millions of Americans are now walking for the health of it!*

Walking is the most popular form of physical activity. Today, walking continues to ride a wave of popularity that draws its strength from a rediscovery of walking's flexibility, pleasures, and health-giving qualities. While other activities generate more conversation and media coverage, none of them approaches walking in number of participants. Approximately half of the adults in the United States claim they walk regularly. Each year the number is increasing.

While activities such as tennis, skiing, swimming, and others have gained great popularity over the years, walking has been widely practiced as a recreational and fitness activity throughout recorded history. For example, Presidents Lincoln, Jefferson, and Truman were avid walkers.

Walking is one of the safest and most effective forms of exercise to improve health, and develop and maintain physical fitness. Physicians, physical therapists, mental health counselors, and other medical professionals have long realized the value of walking for physical, psychological, spiritual, and social well-being.

## HEALTHY PEOPLE 2010

*Healthy People 2010* is a document written by health experts that presents a vision to bring improved health to all people in the United States. Meeting the objectives of *Healthy People 2010* represents a challenge to put prevention into practice by choosing healthy lifestyle choices.

Walking figures prominently in *Healthy People 2010* by directly relating to goal number one: *To help all individuals of all ages increase life expectancy and improve quality of life.*

More Americans are walking to improve their health and fitness.

**Life expectancy** is the average number of years people born in a given year are expected to live based on a set of age-specific death rates. In the early 1900s, life expectancy was only 47.3 years. A baby born today can expect to live 77 years. How long would you like to live?

According to the National Health Interview Survey, approximately 40 percent of adults aged 18 years and older engage in very little or no leisure-time physical activity. One objective of *Healthy People 2010* is to lower this percent to 20 percent. Walking, a simple and easy form of physical activity, is a key strategy to get more individuals to become active in their leisure-time pursuits.

**Quality of life** reflects a general sense of happiness and satisfaction with your life. Walking, when performed on a regular basis, can lead to an increased number of healthy days, months, and years added to your life. This means that if you can be physically active as you live your life, you will have more days of health and happiness and less days of illness and suffering. Is this important to you?

## THE SURGEON GENERAL'S REPORT: PHYSICAL ACTIVITY AND HEALTH

This new report summarizes what has been discovered about physical activity and health. Among its major findings:

- people who are usually inactive can improve their health and well-being by becoming even moderately active on a regular basis.
- physical activity need not be strenuous to achieve health benefits.
- greater health benefits can be achieved by increasing the amount of physical activity through duration, frequency, or intensity.

▶ **Healthy People 2010**
A document of public health opportunities to bring improved health to all people.

▶ **Fitness Walking**
The type of walking that produces measurable health benefits.

▶ **Life Expectancy**
The average number of years people born in a given year are expected to live based on a set of age-specific death rates.

▶ **Quality of Life**
Reflects a general sense of happiness and satisfaction with your life.

▶ **Volksmarch**
A noncompetitive 6-mile walk.

▶ **Volksport**
An association that promotes health, fun, and fellowship through noncompetitive walking (volksmarching) and other sporting events for everyone.

The report also found that 60 percent of adults do not achieve the recommended amount of regular physical activity. In fact, 25 percent of adults are not active at all. According to the Centers for Disease Control and Prevention, inactivity is comparable to smoking a pack of cigarettes a day. In other words, being sedentary is an unhealthy behavior pattern that can lead to serious health consequences. Other findings from this report are found in chapter 2.

The Surgeon General's Report should certainly encourage people to become more active. Many new exercisers will choose walking as their exercise to become fit and shed the couch potato lifestyle—adding to the millions who are already walking.

The following section will define fitness walking and provide indicators that we are experiencing a walking trend.

## WHAT IS FITNESS WALKING?

**Fitness walking** refers to the type of walking that produces health and fitness benefits. For you to be considered a fitness walker, you should walk briskly enough, long enough, and often enough to produce the desireable health and fitness benefits. In addition, you should give proper attention to correct walking techniques, which will be discussed in chapter 8.

## WALKING EVENTS

There are over 10,000 walking events held every year, and this number is increasing. Volksmarching has become popular. A **volksmarch** is a noncompetitive 6-mile (10-kilometer) walk that you can do with your class, a club, your family, your pet, or by yourself. Trails are selected for safety, scenic interest, historic areas, and walkability and take about two hours to complete.

Voluntary health agencies such as the March of Dimes and the American Diabetes Association conduct annual walking events to raise money. Promoters of many events that were for runners only now encourage walkers to enter. There has also been an increase in the number of racewalking events in our country. Racewalking has been an Olympic event since 1908.

## WALKING CLUBS

Walking clubs are being formed all over the country. "The Walkers and Talkers" and "The Striders" are the names of two clubs that have turned fitness walking into an enjoyable social activity. There are now over 500 **volksport** clubs throughout the United States that promote health, fun, and fellowship through noncompetitive walking and sporting events for everyone. To form a walking or volksport at your school or in your community see Appendix B. It's a healthy way to spend time with others.

The number of colleges and universities offering fitness walking courses is rising.

## FITNESS WALKING COURSES IN COLLEGES AND UNIVERSITIES

There is a growing trend among colleges and universities to offer a walking class for credit. Hundreds of institutions of higher learning provide such a course. With the increasing trend in walking, experts predict classes in fitness walking will spread to every school.

## MALL WALKING

At many indoor shopping malls throughout the United States, walkers are allowed to exercise before the stores open or during normal hours of operation. This activity is known as **mall walking.** It has provided many walkers with a comfortable and dependable place to exercise all year. Mall walking offers the additional attractions of personal safety and group participation.

## FITNESS WALKING SHOES

The shoe industry provides further evidence of the walking trend. Many years ago it was difficult to find a good pair of walking shoes, but now most shoe companies make them. Some companies are including the design features of their

Mall walking has become popular as a safe, climate-controlled fitness activity.

fitness walking shoes in their dress shoes, so that it is possible to wear comfortable shoes all day.

## FITNESS WALKING INFORMATION

There has been an increase in the amount of fitness walking information that is available. This information has appeared on the Internet and in magazines, books, and brochures. It has also appeared on television, radio, videotape, and audiocassettes. Resources for fitness walking can be found in Appendix B.

## WALKING TOURS

All over the world, tours are being promoted for walking enthusiasts. Numerous companies offer vacation packages in which two legs are better than four wheels. Walkers can experience the Swiss Alps, the rural footpaths of England, or they can view the wildlife, wildflowers, and spectacular scenery of the Rockies (see Appendix B).

Numerous shoe companies make walking shoes.

## FITNESS WALKING—AN IDEAL FORM OF PHYSICAL ACTIVITY

In an age of high-tech exercise machines, why all of this interest in a form of exercise as old as the human race? There may be as many reasons for this interest as there are fitness walkers; however, when all reasons are considered, people are interested in fitness walking because it is an enjoyable and simple way to improve their health.

Fitness walking can be an escape from a high-tech lifestyle. There is no need for machines, videos, or expensive club memberships. You are not excluded from fitness walking because of your age, body type, or skill level. Plus, walking is convenient—you can walk almost anywhere and almost any time.

Fitness walking is a versatile form of physical activity. The pace can be slow to start and gradually increased as conditioning improves. The techniques are not difficult to learn, and there are several types of walking to choose from: strolling, everyday walking, hiking, backpacking, adventure walking, snowshoeing,

There are several types of walking to choose from: from strolling to racewalking.

stairwalking, fitness walking, and racewalking. You can probably think of other types, all of which allow you to find the best workout for your age, interest, and fitness level.

For these reasons and many others, health professionals are recommending fitness walking as an excellent form of physical activity for all ages.

## CAN WALKING IMPROVE PHYSICAL FITNESS?

For years, it was thought that walking would not provide enough physical activity to produce a cardiovascular benefit; however, scientific research has proven that fitness walkers are able to reach the exercise intensity necessary to improve cardiovascular fitness. When you use correct walking techniques, fitness walking involves most of the muscles in your body. Walking briskly increases the demand for oxygen, which makes your circulatory and respiratory systems work harder than usual, improving the functioning of your heart and lungs.

## IS WALKING SLOW AND BORING?

Of course not! Walking can be fast and interesting. In 1989, Andrey Perlov walked 50 kilometers (31 miles) in 3 hours, 37 minutes, and 41 seconds. That is a 7 minute per mile pace for 31 miles.

Fitness walkers generally walk a mile in about 12 to 17 minutes. Using proper form, with accelerated arm and leg swings, speed can be dramatically increased.

With a positive attitude, walking can be an exciting adventure. There are many entertaining things you can do while you walk. You could listen to a tape player to learn something new, listen to your favorite music, listen to the news, talk with friends and family, sing, solve personal problems, explore new areas, appreciate nature, pray, or meditate. Another suggestion for spicing up your walking routine is to play games. For example, count how many other walkers you see, remember all 50 states and their capitals, or go on a fantasy trip.

## IS WALKING ONLY FOR THE OLD AND INJURED?

It is true that fitness walking is an excellent form of physical activity for older people, for cardiac patients, and for those who have been injured. However, fitness walking is a safe and effective form of physical activity for young, healthy individuals who want to become more fit.

## SUMMARY

- Walking is the most popular form of physical activity.
- Walking is one of the safest and most effective forms of exercise to improve health and develop and maintain physical fitness.
- Walking figures prominently in *Healthy People 2010* by increasing life expectancy and improving quality of life.
- According to the Surgeon General's Report on *Physical Activity and Health*, 60 percent of adults do not achieve the recommended amount of regular physical activity.
- Fitness walking refers to the type of walking that produces health and fitness benefits. It should be done often enough, long enough, and hard enough to receive measurable gains.
- Walking events, clubs, classes, shoes, tours, information, and the popularity of mall walking are indicators of the walking trend.
- Fitness walking can be considered an ideal form of physical activity because of its simplicity, enjoyment, and relationship to physical fitness.
- Fitness walking is an excellent activity for all ages.

# Assessment 1-1

_____    _____    _____
Name                                          Section              Date

    The purpose of this assessment is to observe the popularity of fitness walking.

    See how many people you can find walking for exercise. Look in your neighborhood, local parks, outdoor tracks, walking and jogging trails, and other likely places.

    Count the number of people you see walking for exercise during a 30-minute period. Record the number here.

_____ Number of people I observed walking during a 30-minute period.

    Were you surprised at the number of people you observed walking during the 30-minute period? Explain.

**Yes**   **No**

☐    ☐

# CHAPTER 2

## BENEFITS OF FITNESS WALKING

---

## OBJECTIVES

*After reading this chapter, you should be able to do the following:*

- Recognize the importance of regular exercise as part of a healthy lifestyle.
- Explain why aerobic exercise is important.
- List at least three reasons why fitness walking is an excellent aerobic exercise.

---

### KEY TERMS

*While reading this chapter, you will become familiar with the following terms:*

▶ Aerobic

▶ Exercise

▶ Sedentary

## WHY EXERCISE?

The leading causes of death in the United States are related to lifestyle (see tables 2-1 and 2-2). One harmful lifestyle behavior is **sedentary** living. If you have an inactive lifestyle, there will be a decline in your body's ability to function. If you allow this deterioration to continue, eventually one of your organ systems will not be able to perform its life-sustaining function. When this occurs, you will experience a life-threatening illness or death.

Long before death, however, there may be years of "not feeling very well"— nothing definite, no specific symptoms. The feeling that life is difficult rather than enjoyable, that it is all you can do to plow through another day—these are feelings frequently expressed by people in poor physical condition.

The good news is that a moderate amount of **exercise** on a regular basis will improve the functioning of your body. Exercise can help you look better, feel better, and enjoy life.

## WHY AEROBIC EXERCISE?

You are an aerobic organism. The term **aerobic** (a-rō′-bik) describes life forms that require oxygen. You could live weeks without food, days without water, but only minutes without oxygen. How well your body operates depends on your ability to get oxygen to every living cell.

Oxygen is brought into your body with the air you breathe into your lungs. Approximately one-fifth of normal, unpolluted air is oxygen. Some of the oxygen that enters your lungs is transferred into your blood. Your heart then pumps the oxygenated blood to all of your cells.

**TABLE 2-1**

**Leading Causes of Death in the United States (1998)**

- Heart Disease: **724,859**
- Cancer: **541,532**
- Stroke: **158,448**
- Chronic Obstructive Pulmonary Disease: **112,584**
- Accidents: **97,835**
- Pneumonia/Influenza: **91,871**
- Diabetes: **64,751**
- Suicide: **30,575**
- Nephritis, nephrotic syndrome, and nephrosis: **26,182**
- Chronic Liver Disease and Cirrhosis: **25,192**

Data from the National Vital Statistics Reports, Vol. 48, No. 11.

**TABLE 2-2**
**Actual Causes of Death in the United States**

| Cause | Estimated Number of Deaths |
|---|---|
| Tobacco | 400,000 |
| Diet/activity patterns | 300,000 |
| Alcohol | 100,000 |
| Microbial agents | 90,000 |
| Toxic agents | 60,000 |
| Firearms | 35,000 |
| Sexual behavior | 30,000 |
| Motor vehicles | 25,000 |
| Illicit use of drugs | 20,000 |

From J.M. McGinnis and W.H. Foege, Actual Causes of Death in the United States, *Journal of the American Medical Association,* Vol. 270, p. 2208, © 1993, American Medical Association.

Any lifestyle behavior that reduces the functioning of your respiratory or circulatory system reduces your ability to get life-sustaining oxygen to your cells. Sedentary living reduces your ability to deliver oxygen to all parts of your body. This decline in oxygen delivery could be considered a slow form of suffocation and results in "not feeling very well."

If this deterioration continues, eventually you will only be able to take in enough oxygen to sustain your life in a resting state. This does not leave any room for adjustment to an increased demand, such as a physical or an emotional emergency. A poorly conditioned person may experience a sudden demand for increased oxygen delivery. Since his or her body is not capable of delivering more oxygen to the heart muscle, now working harder than normal, some of the oxygen-starved heart muscle tissue may die. The affected tissue can no longer contract; therefore, the heart may not be able to continue to pump oxygenated blood to any of the other living cells of the body. This is a simplified explanation of one type of heart attack. Without a continuous supply of life-sustaining oxygen, the other cells of the body cannot survive.

► **Aerobic**
Requiring oxygen to live and thrive.

► **Exercise**
Bodily exertion that is done to develop, maintain, or improve physical fitness.

► **Sedentary**
A way of living characterized by only minimal physical activity.

Six major aerobic activities: (a) walking, (b) swimming, (c) step aerobics, (d) water aerobics, (e) bicycling, and (f) jogging.

Since you are an aerobic organism, exercises that improve your ability to obtain and use oxygen (aerobic exercises) are beneficial. They stimulate the development of your oxygen delivery system. Aerobic exercises use large muscle groups in a rhythmic and continuous manner. Listed in the accompanying box are some of the benefits of aerobic exercise.

## Benefits of Aerobic Exercise

The following benefits have been reported as a result of a moderate amount of aerobic exercise performed on a regular basis. All of these benefits are still under investigation. Some have been studied more thoroughly than others. Biological adaptation to exercise is a gradual process that requires consistent and long-term participation.

**Heart**

—Increased strength of the heart muscle
—Increased stroke volume
—Increased cardiac output
—Increased heart volume
—Decreased resting heart rate
—Decreased exercise heart rate at a standard workload
—Decreased risk of cardiovascular disease
—Decreased risk of heart attack
—Decreased severity of heart attack if one does occur
—Increased chance of surviving a heart attack if one does occur

**Blood**

—Increased blood flow
—Increased total blood volume
—Increased number of red blood cells
—Increased oxygen-carrying capacity of the blood
—Increased high-density lipoproteins (HDL)
—Increased ability to extract oxygen from the blood
—Decreased harmful blood fats
—Decreased total cholesterol

**Blood Vessels**

—Increased size of capillaries
—Increased number of open capillaries
—Increased peripheral circulation
—Increased coronary circulation
—Decreased resting blood pressure for some individuals
—Decreased risk of atherosclerosis

*Continued*

## Benefits of Aerobic Exercise

*Continued from p. 17*

### Lungs
—Increased minute volume of air
—Increased rate of breathing during exercise
—Increased volume per breath during exercise

### Body Fat
—Decreased total body fat
—Decreased percent body fat
—Maintenance of healthy body-fat level
—Decreased appetite if exercise is performed just before a meal
—Decreased total body weight

### Muscle
—Increased lean body weight
—Increased muscle tissue
—Increased muscle strength
—Increased muscle endurance

### Bone
—Increased bone density
—Increased bone and joint strength
—Decreased risk of osteoporosis

### Connective Tissue
—Increased tendon, ligament, and joint strength

### Endurance
—Increased work efficiency
—Increased sports performance
—Increased ability to use oxygen
—Increased physical ability to meet emergency situations
—Increased recovery after hard work
—Increased cardiovascular endurance
—Increased functioning of oxygen supply organ systems

## Benefits of Aerobic Exercise

**Resistance to Disease**

—Increased resistance
—Increased health

**Appearance**

—Improved appearance
—Improved posture
—Decreased waistline

**Stress**

—Decreased emotional stress

**Psychological**

—Increased self-concept
—Increased positive attitude, positive feeling
—Increased self-confidence
—Increased self-discipline
—Increased independence for many older citizens
—Decreased depression
—Increased soundness of sleep
—Decreased mental tension
—Increased social interaction with healthy people
—Increased resistance to fatigue
—Increased feeling of success
—Increased enjoyment of leisure time
—Increased enjoyment of work
—Increased quality of life, sense of well-being

# WHY FITNESS WALKING?

Fitness walking is an excellent aerobic exercise for many reasons.

### ▶ Lifetime Exercise

To get the greatest benefit from exercise, it must be consistent and lifelong, 12 months a year, every year. Because it is a low-impact activity, walking can be enjoyed by people of all ages.

### ▶ Almost Everyone Can Participate

Walking has few restrictions. Almost everyone can participate in fitness walking. No special sports skills are necessary to achieve a beneficial amount of exercise.

If you are overweight, walking is ideal because it puts less strain on your bones and joints than some of the other aerobic activities.

### ▶ Natural and Safe Exercise

Walking is one of the most natural exercises for the human body. Your body was designed for movement, not inactivity.

Walking is a convenient and enjoyable method of transportation.

Walking is also a safe exercise. Many former joggers have converted to fitness walking. The force of landing on each foot during jogging is about three and one-half to four times your body weight. In contrast, the force of landing on each foot during walking is about one to one and one-half times your body weight. Therefore, joint and muscle injuries are less likely to occur with a walking program.

## ▶ Inexpensive

Fitness walking does not require expensive facilities, equipment, or membership. The most expensive and important equipment for fitness walking is a good pair of walking shoes. However, such shoes can be worn in a variety of situations and over a long period. Therefore, considering the cost per hour of use, walking shoes are less expensive than most other exercise equipment.

As fitness walking continues its rapid growth in popularity, creative people will develop innovative products, facilities, clothing, equipment, and memberships that will find a market. If you enjoy these new products and services, have a desire for them, and can afford them, that's fine—but remember that they are not necessary for you to gain the benefits from fitness walking.

## ▶ Fat Loss

From 1991 through 1998, obesity in the United States increased in every state, for both men and women, across all age categories, all races, and all educational levels. Fitness walking is an excellent way to decrease body fat. Since so many people are interested in losing excess body fat, chapter 10 in this book is devoted to this important benefit of fitness walking.

## ▶ Easier to Start and Stick With

Walking is a familiar activity, one in which you already have some skill. Since you know how to do it and can do it almost anywhere, it is relatively easy to start a walking exercise program.

The dropout rate for fitness walking is lower than for other exercise programs. Walking is convenient and accessible, and it can be used as a form of transportation. Walking can be combined with other enjoyable activities, such as sightseeing and carrying on a conversation. Because walking is more enjoyable than some of the other fitness activities, you are more likely to stick with your exercise program.

## ▶ Posture

Fitness walking promotes good posture by strengthening many of your muscles. Good posture allows you to function more effectively, expending a minimum amount of energy. With good posture, there is less strain on your muscles,

# Fitness Tip

## Your Walking Plan

- Set walking goals that are realistic for you. You'll be more likely to continue if you do.
- Be moderate in your exercise. Don't try to walk too fast, too long, or too often—especially when you're starting.
- Make walking a regular part of your week. Schedule a specific time to walk, such as in the morning, after classes, or before dinner.

tendons, ligaments, and joints. Good posture also conveys an impression of alertness, confidence, and attractiveness.

## ▶ Social Activity

Walking is an excellent family and group activity. It can be a social activity and a fitness activity at the same time. Whereas runners often have difficulty maintaining a conversation while they exercise, walkers are more likely to maintain a conversation due to the lower intensity of many walking programs.

Walking provides an excellent opportunity for family members and friends to spend regular time together. It provides a time to discuss personal and family needs, wants, goals, and dreams. Instead of going out for dinner, dessert, or a drink, which all add calories, why not go out for a walk together, which will burn calories?

## ▶ Get Fit for Sports

You can start slowly with fitness walking and gradually build to a high level of fitness. For people who have not been exercising, walking is recommended as a starter program to prepare for participation in sports.

## ▶ Rehabilitation of Injuries

Walking can be an excellent exercise to help an individual recover from injuries, especially leg injuries. When muscles are not used, they atrophy (decrease in size and strength). Walking can be an important exercise in the recovery process because the intensity of the exercise and the workload placed on the injured tissue can be controlled to a greater extent than in many other exercises. Walking helps rebuild or maintain muscle tissue as the injury heals.

Family and friends can enjoy walking together.

## ▶ Cardiac Rehabilitation

Walking is the primary exercise in many cardiac rehabilitation programs. It is a good exercise for those recovering from heart attacks because walking is an exercise that they

- are familiar with,
- are not afraid of,
- can continue for the rest of their lives,
- can easily monitor,
- can start at a low level, and
- can progressively increase.

Walking puts heart attack victims on their feet again. It helps them regain some control of their lives and feel optimistic about the future.

## ▶ Exercise During Pregnancy

Walking is one of the safest and best exercises during pregnancy. When they find out they are pregnant, many women stop all physical activity and become deconditioned in preparation for the most demanding physical activity of their lives. When they do finally give birth, they are in their weakest physical condition as a result of nine months of deconditioning. Adequate exercise and good nutrition bring many benefits to the developing child as well as to the mother.

Fitness walking is a good exercise for pregnant women because it is a low-impact activity. Also, the intensity level can be easily monitored and adjusted to the fairly rapid biological changes that occur during pregnancy.

Walking is an excellent exercise during and after pregnancy.

## ▶  Exercise After Pregnancy

Walking is an excellent exercise after pregnancy. A new mother can start slowly and progress gradually as her fitness level improves. She can begin to lose excess body fat she may have gained during pregnancy. Walking after pregnancy also promotes cardiovascular endurance—an important attribute for a new parent.

Walking is not only a good exercise, it is also good for stress management. It provides an opportunity to enjoy being outdoors. A new mother can take her baby along in a stroller; the stimulation of new surroundings is good for young children. She might choose to leave the baby with another caregiver for 30 to 60 minutes while taking an exercise break.

## ▶  Fits in with Your Daily Routine

You can choose to walk at a time that best fits your schedule. Some people prefer to walk early in the morning to start the day. Others prefer to walk late at night. Still others choose to walk at noon or during breaks. These are only a few of the ways people fit walking into their daily routine.

Walking can fit into anyone's daily routine.

## ▶ Mental Benefits

Walking is good for your brain as well as the rest of your body. A University of Illinois study of sedentary people who were 60 and older found that those who started a walking program scored up to 25 percent higher on memory and judgement tests.

## ▶ Psychological Benefits

Regular fitness walkers have come to appreciate the value of this exercise for their psychological well-being. Many walkers report that the psychological benefits from walking are just as important, if not more important, than the physical benefits. Figure 2-1 highlights some of the major psychological benefits from a regular program of fitness walking.

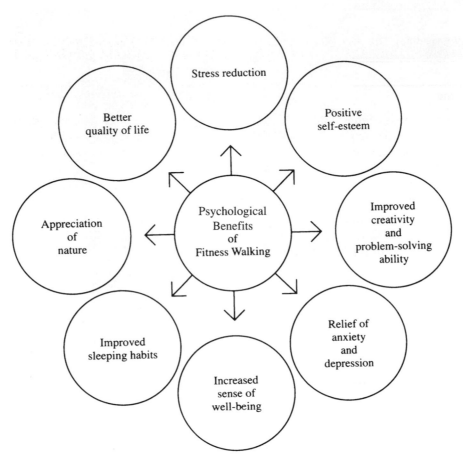

**FIGURE 2-1**  The psychological benefits of fitness walking.

## SUMMARY

- Moderate exercise done on a regular basis is an important part of promoting and maintaining good health.
- Regular aerobic exercise produces many benefits—physical, mental, and psychological.
- Fitness walking is an excellent aerobic exercise that can be done by most people.
- One way to decrease excess body fat is through regular fitness walking.
- Walking is the primary exercise used in many cardiac rehabilitation programs.
- One of the safest and best exercises to do during and after a pregnancy is walking.

# Assessment 2-1

Name                    Section          Date

The purpose of this activity is to determine the reasons for your participation in a fitness walking program. List the benefits you would like to receive from your fitness walking program. Don't evaluate them at this time; just list them as quickly as you can think of them. When you can't think of any more to list, go back and place a check next to the three benefits you most hope to achieve. Of those three, which one is the most important to you?

Check off your top three benefits.

_____  1. _____

_____  2. _____

_____  3. _____

_____  4. _____

_____  5. _____

_____  6. _____

_____  7. _____

_____  8. _____

_____  9. _____

_____ 10. _____

Which benefit is most important to you? _____

# CHAPTER 3

# CLOTHING AND EQUIPMENT

## OBJECTIVES

*After reading this chapter, you should be able to do the following:*

- Explain what to look for in a good walking shoe.
- Describe how to dress for fitness walking in different weather conditions.
- Identify equipment that might make fitness walking safer and more enjoyable.

## KEY TERMS

*While reading this chapter, you will become familiar with the following terms:*

- ► Inner Sole
- ► Mid-Sole
- ► Motion Control
- ► Outer Sole
- ► Pulsemeter (Heart Rate Monitor)

- ► Racewalking Shoes
- ► Rocker-Shaped Sole
- ► Sauna Suit
- ► Upper Shoe
- ► Walking Shoes

One of the advantages of fitness walking is cost. You don't need to spend a lot of money on special clothing and equipment. Some activities, such as skiing and scuba diving, require expensive equipment that you might use only once or twice a year. Most fitness walking clothing and equipment is inexpensive and can be used every day.

The most important piece of clothing or equipment you can buy for fitness walking is a good pair of **walking shoes.** They may seem expensive when you first look at the selling price; however, if you take the time to calculate the cost per hour of use and the value of your health, you will find high-quality walking shoes to be a good investment.

## WALKING SHOES

Approximately 87 percent of Americans have suffered from foot problems. Many of these foot problems are caused by poor shoe design, shoes that do not fit properly, or shoes that are worn out. When shopping for shoes, spend a little extra time and money to get good quality and a proper fit.

When shopping for fitness walking shoes, be sure to allow enough time. Do not try to do it in five minutes. Be a good comparison shopper. Try on at least three different brands and as many styles as possible. Even if a shoe is ranked as the best, or the most popular, it may not fit you as comfortably as another brand or model.

When you try on walking shoes, test them on a hard surface instead of the padded carpet commonly found in shoe stores. This test will help you determine the amount of cushion and comfort the shoes provide.

### ▶ Outer Sole

Figure 3-1 shows the components of a good walking shoe. The **outer sole** is the material on the bottom of a shoe. It should be made from a durable material. A good walking shoe has a **rocker-shaped sole,** which helps your foot rock forward from heel to toe. Walking shoes have a tread design for traction; however, it is not as deep as commonly found on running shoes.

Some people experience undesirable foot motion when they walk. These undesirable foot movements could result in injury when participating in a highly repetitive activity like fitness walking. Therefore, many shoe companies now make shoe models with **motion control.** Motion control is designed into the shoe to keep your foot moving from heel to toe without excessive movement toward the inside or outside edge of your foot. Look for a knowledgeable athletic shoe professional who can help you select the best shoes for your feet.

▶ **Mid-Sole**

The **mid-sole** is a cushioning layer between the outer and inner soles. Since the primary purpose of the mid-sole is to absorb shock, it can be made from a variety of materials and designed in many different ways.

There is no exact way for most people to determine when the mid-sole has lost its ability to absorb shock. The outer sole and upper part of the shoe may look fine, but, if the mid-sole has lost its resiliency, it is time to get a new pair of walking shoes.

▶ **Inner Sole**

The **inner sole** makes direct contact with your foot. This sole should include an arch support and a heel cup. Some shoes have an arch support that can be added to, or removed from, the inner sole. The inner sole may also provide additional air or gel cushioning.

The inner sole can be removed from many walking shoes. There are three advantages to this. One is to let the inner sole air out after a workout. A second is that it can be replaced if it wears out. A third is that a podiatrist or an orthopedic doctor can make an inner sole designed for your foot.

---

▶ **Inner Sole**
The bottom portion of a shoe that makes direct contact with your foot.

▶ **Mid-Sole**
The cushioning layer between the outer and inner soles of a shoe.

▶ **Motion Control**
Features designed into a shoe to reduce or eliminate undesirable foot movements.

▶ **Outer Sole**
The material on the bottom of a shoe.

▶ **Pulsemeter or Heart Rate Monitor**
A piece of equipment that displays your heart rate.

▶ **Racewalking Shoes**
Lighter weight walking shoes designed for racing.

▶ **Rocker-Shaped Sole**
A shoe sole that is rounded from front to back so you can roll your foot from heel to toe as you walk.

▶ **Sauna Suit**
Exercise clothing made of nonporous material that will not allow heat and perspiration to escape.

▶ **Upper Shoe**
The top part of a shoe above the sole.

▶ **Walking Shoes**
Shoes designed specifically for walking.

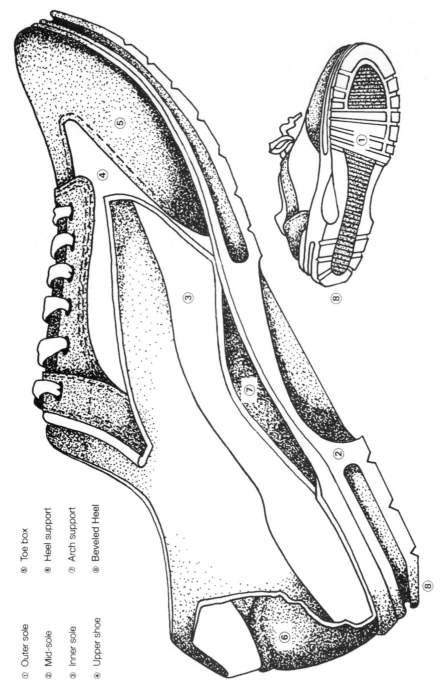

① Outer sole    ⑤ Toe box

② Mid-sole    ⑥ Heel support

③ Inner sole    ⑦ Arch support

④ Upper shoe    ⑧ Beveled Heel

**FIGURE 3-1** Important components of a good quality walking shoe.

## ▶ Upper Shoe

The **upper shoe** is often made of leather or mesh because they are durable, supple materials. The toe box portion of the shoe should be wide enough so that the front part of your foot can spread out. This will allow you to push off with all of your toes.

The heel of the upper shoe should include a stiff material to provide support and to hold your foot in position. Good walking shoes often have a notch at the top of the heel support to minimize irritation of the Achilles tendon.

Some walking shoes also have reflective material on the upper shoe as a safety measure for those who walk in the dark.

## ▶ Size and Comfort

Try on both shoes. One of your feet may be longer than the other. Purchase shoes that are comfortable for the longest foot. You may need to wear an extra sock on the smaller foot if there is a big difference.

You may find that different brands of shoes fit differently, even if the sizes marked on the shoes are the same. Also, the size of your feet may have changed since your last shoe purchase. If you choose to buy your walking shoes through a mail order company, make sure it has a good return policy.

Walking shoes should not require a "break in" period. However, it is still a good idea to alternate your old shoes with your new shoes for a couple weeks. This allows your feet to adjust to the change gradually.

Walking shoes should fit comfortably, not too tight or too loose. They need to be long enough and wide enough. Fitness walking shoes should be at least one-fourth of an inch longer than your big toe, and your feet should not feel squeezed into a shoe that is too narrow. Do not sacrifice comfort for name brand, style, or sale price. It is important that your walking shoes be comfortable.

## ▶ Flexibility

All three soles and the upper shoe should bend at the ball of your foot. A good walking shoe should be flexible at this point.

A good walking shoe is flexible.

## ▶ Weight

**Racewalking shoes** tend to be lighter than training shoes. A few ounces of additional weight might make a difference in a race. However, most fitness walkers prefer training shoes that are more durable.

## ▶ Quality

Look carefully at walking shoes. Is the shoe made from quality materials? Is it put together well? Is the stitching done carefully? Is the upper shoe securely fastened to the mid-sole?

Fitness walking shoes are an investment in your health. Invest wisely; insist on quality.

## ▶ Shopping Guide

In *Walking* magazine, Brad Ketchum, Jr. and Tom Brunick offered the following tips for selecting walking shoes.

1. **Toe box.** The most important thing a walker needs in a shoe is a good fit, and fit begins with the toe box. Look for a rounded, roomy toe compartment with three-dimensional space—shoes that taper or recede toward the toes might literally cramp your (walking) style. There's no need to sacrifice fit for fashion.
2. **Lacing.** A good lacing system can customize the fit of a walking shoe. Almost all models come with variable-width or dual lacing, which includes at least one set of double eyelets near the top of the shoe. Walkers with narrow feet should use the outer eyelets to pull the upper tight; those with wide feet can use the inner eyelets for more room. Among the latest lacing features are plastic straps and stretch panels to further perfect the fit.
3. **Interiors.** Look for three features inside a walking shoe: a padded heel collar to reduce chafing; a padded tongue to protect the forefoot; and a smooth, absorbent lining. Also check the inner sole. As previously mentioned, most are removable so that they can be aired out or replaced.
4. **Heel cup.** The heel cup provides support in a walking shoe. Most shoes have plastic heel cups sewn inside the upper. Many also have smaller, external "stabilizers," which create a stable platform to keep your heel from rolling from side to side. For more support, look for a heel cup that extends all the way around the side of the shoe toward the arch.
5. **Rocker profile.** Look for a natural, heel-to-toe curve. When the shoe is placed on a table, neither the heel nor the toe should touch the surface. Models with extreme rocker bottoms will rest on the middle of their outer soles. The heel should also be slightly beveled for proper heel strike.

Some walkers prefer to have two pairs of walking shoes. Switching between two pairs of shoes gives your feet a break from wearing only one pair. Also, if the shoes get wet, they will have time to dry between workouts.

## CLOTHING

Clothing for fitness walking should be comfortable, allow for freedom of movement, and make you feel good about your appearance. Socks should absorb perspiration. For extra comfort, you may want to wear two pairs. Another option would be to buy socks that have extra cushioning in the heel and forefoot area. This extra cushioning may reduce friction and help prevent blisters. A sports bra for women, and an athletic supporter for men, provide firm support and generally make fitness walking more comfortable. However, this is a matter of personal comfort and preference.

### ▶ Hot Weather Clothing

Light-colored and loose-fitting clothes are cooler than dark, tight clothes during hot weather. Light-colored clothing reflects some of the sun's rays, and loose-fitting clothing allows air to circulate next to your skin.

Walking shorts should allow free and easy movement. Light-weight shorts with built-in briefs add support with little increase in bulk. Shorts that are made of thick material might have a bulky inseam that could rub on the inside of your thighs. Another advantage of light-weight shorts is that they dry quickly. It is possible to rinse them out after each workout and have them clean and dry for the next day.

Loose-fitting shirts made of natural fabrics, such as cotton, absorb perspiration and allow air next to your skin.

A good hot-weather walking hat should have a raised crown with vents to allow air to circulate between the top of the hat and your head. Some people prefer a visor. In sunny weather, the brim of the hat or visor should protect your eyes and forehead from the harmful rays of the sun. On hot, sunny days a hat helps prevent headaches and fatigue. It is also a good idea to wear sunscreen on days when your skin will be exposed to the sun.

Any time you are walking in the heat be aware of the dangers of hyperthemia (overheating) that can cause heat cramps, heat exhaustion, and heat stroke. Some of the symptoms include thirst, headache, dizziness, pallor, nausea, vomiting, disorientation, and extremely fast heart rate. These symptoms are somewhat progressive in their severity. Be aware, pay attention, and catch it early before the symptoms get worse. If you are exercising in the heat and begin to experience these symptoms stop exercising, get out of the sun, and get into an air-conditioned building or some other cool place. Drink water slowly, but frequently, as opposed to drinking a large amount quickly. If you don't begin to feel better within 30 minutes, seek medical attention.

Hot and cold weather clothing.

## ▶ Cold Weather Clothing

For fitness walking in cold weather, dress in layers of clothing. This will allow you to remove layers to regulate your body temperature as you walk. Keeping warm while exercising in cold weather is not as much of a problem as you might think. Approximately 75 percent of the energy released during muscle contraction is heat energy; therefore, your muscles produce a lot of heat during exercise. You can use your layers of clothing to control how much heat you want next to your skin.

The first layer of clothing next to your skin should be made of a material that will keep you warm and dry. It should draw moisture away from your skin; it is difficult to stay warm if you are wet. This layer should be a loose-weave fabric with air spaces that can hold warm air next to your body.

The next layer on your upper body might be a long-sleeved t-shirt or a turtle-neck. On top of that, add a wool pullover or a sweatshirt.

The top layer could be a cotton sweatsuit or a garment made of a synthetic fabric, depending on the weather conditions. If the weather is wet, the outer layer should be waterproof. If the weather is cold and windy, the outer layer should serve as a windbreaker.

Warm-up suits with air vents enhance evaporation, thus reducing the moisture content inside the suit. These warm-up suits hold most of the heat in while allowing the moisture to escape.

A knit hat is recommended for cold weather. Wool is popular. A hat or hood helps hold in body heat. As much as two-thirds of your body heat can be lost from your head if it is not covered.

Gloves or mittens should be worn during fitness walking because the fingers are especially vulnerable to the cold. A woven material allows perspiration to be drawn away from your skin, whereas a solid synthetic material allows perspiration to accumulate. Natural fabrics, such as cotton or wool, work well.

## ▶ Body Suits

Body suits made of lycra or lycra blend material are available. They conform to the shape of your body like a layer of skin. If a body suit is comfortable, if it does not restrict your movement, and if you feel good in it, this may be a good choice of walking clothing for you.

## ▶ Sauna Suits

Rubber suits or **sauna suits** are dangerous and should not be worn. These suits are made of nonporous material; air and moisture cannot pass through. Sauna suits have elastic at the neck, wrists, waist, and ankles. During exercise, the air between the suit and your skin becomes hot and humid. It is possible to experience extreme heat and humidity inside a sauna suit, even on a comfortable day; thus, heat cramps, heat exhaustion, and heat stroke can occur.

Some people wear sauna suits during exercise so they will sweat more. Heavy sweating may result in a rapid, but temporary, weight loss. However, the pounds lost are due to fluid loss, not fat loss. The fluid and weight are quickly regained with any food or liquid intake. This is an unhealthy and ineffective way to attempt to lose weight. A healthy way to lose weight and body fat is to use more calories than you consume over time.

# EQUIPMENT

Fitness walking equipment can make walking safe and enjoyable.

## ▶ Sunglasses

Sunglasses are important to protect your eyes from the harmful direct rays of the sun and from reflected glare. The best sunglasses to use are the ones that provide UV (ultraviolet) protection. As a fitness walker, it is possible to experience dizziness and temporary vision impairment if your eyes are not shielded from direct sunlight.

## ▶ Reflective Material

Some people walk when it is dark. This is especially true during the winter months, when the daylight hours are short. You can put reflective tape on your walking clothes and shoes, and reflective vests are available. If you decide not to use reflective material, at least wear light-colored clothing that can be seen more easily at night.

## ▶ Pulsemeter or Heart Rate Monitor

A **pulsemeter or heart rate monitor** allows you to monitor your heart rate while you are walking. You need to reach a prescribed exercise heart rate to receive an adequate cardiovascular training effect. A pulsemeter can inform you when you have reached your exercise heart rate. It provides feedback that can be used to stay at the correct exercise heart rate for the duration of your walk.

## ▶ Pedometer

A pedometer is a device that measures how far you walk. This is usually done by counting the number of steps you take. On some models, you need to preset your approximate stride length.

## ▶ Backpack and Fanny Packs

Backpacks are useful for one-day hikes and weekend trips. In your backpack, you can carry first aid items, a change of socks, and extra layers of clothing. Waist packs, or fanny packs, are also available to carry small items, such as keys, during your workout.

## ▶ Hand Weights

Hand weights may be carried during fitness walking to increase your muscular effort, energy expenditure, oxygen demand, and heart rate. Beginners should not carry weights. The additional exercise load could be harmful for an unconditioned beginner. Hand weights should only be considered by intermediate or advanced fitness walkers. Even more experienced walkers should start with light hand weights and only progress to heavier hand weights gradually.

## ▶ Walking Sticks and Canes

Some people use walking sticks, poles, and canes when walking. They can serve a dual function of helping maintain balance and self-defense. Walking sticks, poles, and canes may be especially useful to defend yourself against aggressive animals.

## SUMMARY

- A good walking shoe that fits you well is your most important piece of fitness walking clothing and equipment.
- Size and comfort, flexibility, weight, and quality are key considerations in choosing a walking shoe.
- When shopping for walking shoes, you should also consider toe box, lacing, interiors, heel cup, and rocker profile.
- Once you learn to dress appropriately for current weather conditions, fitness walking can be a year-round outdoor fitness activity.
- Equipment such as reflective material, a pulsemeter, and a pedometer could make fitness walking safer and more enjoyable for you.

# Assessment 3-1

Name          Section        Date

Before investing in a pair of walking shoes, visit several stores that carry these shoes. Look carefully at each shoe to evaluate the materials and workmanship. Try on different brands and models so you can feel the difference. Then answer the following questions.

1. Which shoes are made with better quality materials?

2. Which shoes are the cheapest?

3. Which shoes are the most expensive?

4. Which shoes offer the most support?

5. Which shoes offer the most cushion?

6. Which shoes feel the most comfortable?

# CHAPTER 4

# SAFETY

## OBJECTIVES

*After reading this chapter, you should be able to do the following:*

- Explain the safety concerns related to participating in a fitness walking program.
- Discuss the various safety recommendations proposed for fitness walking.
- Identify the basic signs of overtraining.

## KEY TERMS

*While reading this chapter, you will become familiar with the following terms:*

- ► **Dehydration**
- ► **Extreme Weather Conditions**
- ► **Heat Cramps**
- ► **Heat Exhaustion**

- ► **Heat Stroke**
- ► **Hypothermia**
- ► **Overtraining**

Fitness walking has been touted as a lifestyle behavior that contributes to numerous fitness and health benefits. However, to ensure these benefits and to be a safe fitness walker, there are special considerations that deserve mention. Careful attention should be given to the safety concerns highlighted in this chapter.

## LISTEN TO YOUR BODY

Too much exercise the first day can result in unnecessary pain and injury. When you begin an exercise program, start slowly.

Some mild muscle soreness a day or two after beginning a new exercise program is common and can be relieved with static stretching and aerobic exercise. Both of these should be included in your fitness walking workouts.

If you progress slowly into your new exercise program, you should not experience any extreme pain. Pain is generally an indication of injury. If you do experience extreme pain, you should stop exercising and seek medical attention. Learn to listen to your body for feedback about the effects of your fitness walking program. Fitness walking should feel good, and you should look forward to your next session.

## MEDICAL CLEARANCE

People of any age who are not at high risk for serious health problems can safely exercise at a moderate level of intensity without prior medical evaluation. In addition, if you are a male and under 40, or a female under 50, and in good health, physical activity is probably safe for you. If you are over these ages or have health problems (especially high blood pressure, heart disease, obesity, muscle and joint problems), see your physician before starting a walking program. If you're not sure whether you should receive a medical clearance, it's best to be on the safe side and get the green light from your physician.

## WALKING DURING EXTREME WEATHER CONDITIONS

One excuse people use for not exercising on a regular basis is the weather. Although there is a wide range of weather conditions in which fitness walking can be performed, there are also some dangers of exercising in **extreme weather conditions.** If you know the dangers and take precautions, the weather should rarely be used as an excuse for not exercising.

▶ **Hot Weather Walking**

The dangers of physical activity in hot weather should be taken seriously. Physical activity in hot and humid settings can reduce the body's ability to regulate it's temperature. The primary method for the body to regulate temperature is through evaporation of sweat. However, when conditions are humid, it becomes difficult for the body to "cool off" because the air is already saturated with moisture. If water or other replacement fluids are not used, **dehydration** occurs. In turn, the rate of sweating decreases as the body begins to conserve its remaining water. The result of this process can impair performance and lead to various heat-related problems such as **heat cramps, heat exhaustion,** and **heat stroke.** Symptoms include dizziness, nausea, fatigue, headaches, clammy skin, paleness, rapid breathing, lack of sweating, and confusion.

# Fitness Tip

## Treating Heat-Related Problems

The treatment for heat-related problems includes these steps:

- stop exercise
- rest in cool place
- take off unneeded clothing
- drink plenty of water
- use cold towels

---

▶ **Dehydration**
Excessive loss of water from the body, usually from perspiration.

▶ **Extreme Weather Conditions**
Weather-related factors such as hot and cold weather where precautions are necessary.

▶ **Heat Cramps**
Characterized by muscle spasms or twitching of the limbs.

▶ **Heat Exhaustion**
A condition that results in general weakness; fatigue; a drop in blood pressure; blurred vision; occasionally loss of consciousness; and profuse sweating with pale, clammy skin.

▶ **Heat Stroke**
Excessively high body temperature that can lead to an extremely severe condition.

▶ **Hypothermia**
Excessively low body temperature characerized by uncontrollable shivering, coordination loss, and mental confusion.

▶ **Overtraining**
A condition caused by training too much or too intensely and characterized by lack of energy, decreased physical performance, fatigue, depression, aching muscles and joints, and susceptibility to injury.

# Fitness Tip

## Reducing Your Risk of Dehydration

To reduce your risk of dehydration and heat-related problems, follow these guidelines:

- Drink 2 cups or 16 ounces of water before starting your fitness walk.

- Drink 1 cup or 5 to 10 ounces of water every 15 to 20 minutes during your walk.

- After your walk, drink as much water as you want.

Other hot weather precautions include: wear light-colored, loose-fitting clothing; walk during the coolest times of the day; reduce the intensity of your exercise; reduce the duration of your exercise; and rest at regular intervals, preferably in the shade.

▶ **Cold Weather Walking**

Dehydration can also be a problem when exercising during cold weather. When the weather is cold and dry, perspiration evaporates quickly. You should drink plenty of water and avoid diuretic liquids, such as coffee and tea.

In freezing temperatures and windy conditions, frostbite can occur within minutes on your hands, nose, ears, and toes. Be sure these areas are covered with clothing during extremely cold weather. If you are walking during cold weather and notice any tissue that is numb, or turning hard and white, take immediate action. Get indoors, where the air temperature is warmer, and soak the tissue in warm water. Do not use hot water because tissue damage may occur.

Prolonged exposure to the cold, accompanied by excessive loss of body heat, can lead to a life-threatening condition in which your core body temperature drops to a dangerous level. **Hypothermia** is the term for low body temperature. The symptoms of hypothermia include disorientation, sluggishness, slurred speech, and a stumbling gait. Be sure you dress warmly enough to maintain your core body temperature when walking during cold weather.

People with high blood pressure need to keep warm because shivering elevates blood pressure. Angina (chest pain) can also be a result of exposure to the cold. If you have angina, and the air temperature is low, wear a scarf that covers your mouth and nose. If you have any kind of cardiovascular disease, walk indoors when the outdoor temperature drops below 20° F. Mall walking has become popular, especially in colder climates.

Since cold weather is often accompanied by snow and ice, the danger of slipping and falling is increased. It is a good idea to walk where other people will be around to help if you fall.

Drink plenty of fluids before, during, and after exercise.

There is a myth that being in the cold will cause you to catch a cold. It is really viruses from others that are the primary cause of the common cold. These are most frequently found indoors, in warm, recirculated air, where we spend more time when the outside air temperature is low. Being in cold air can dry out the mucous membranes of your mouth and nose, which may make it easier for viruses to penetrate when you go indoors. Therefore, fitness walking during cold weather should not cause you to catch a cold, as long as you enter a relatively virus-free environment when you go indoors.

When exercising in cold weather, it is important to control the amount of heat lost from your body. In addition to dressing in layers of clothing, cover your head and hands. As much as 70 percent of your body heat can be lost from these areas during cold weather if they are not covered.

As long as you are healthy and dress warmly, cold weather should not be an excuse to miss your fitness walking workout.

## ▶ Wet Weather Walking

Many beginning exercisers use wet weather as an excuse to skip their exercise session. Is this necessary? Human skin is waterproof; besides, these same people usually take a shower after exercise and get wet in the process. A large number of experienced fitness walkers and joggers enjoy a workout while it is raining or snowing. Remember how much fun it was to play in the rain when you were a child?

If you want to try to stay dry while walking in the rain, there are waterproof exercise suits available. Some of these water-resistant materials are expensive, but the cost is well worth it if a rain suit will help you stick with your walking program. If you walk vigorously and produce a lot of perspiration, it will not evaporate on a rainy day anyway, because the air is already completely saturated

Walking in the rain can add variety to your fitness program.

with moisture. Therefore, you will be wet from perspiration instead of rain. Walking in the rain or snow is not harmful if you take a warm bath or shower; dry off; and put on warm, dry clothing soon after you finish.

Whereas the rain does not hurt you, lightning certainly could. If there is lightning outdoors, find a way to exercise indoors or wait for the storm to pass.

## DRUGS

There is no place in a health improvement program, such as fitness walking, for the use of recreational drugs.

If you are required to take prescription drugs for your health, consult with your physician before starting an exercise program. Exercise may alter the effects of the medicine.

## CARS

When a car comes near you, look directly into the driver's eyes to determine if the driver has seen you. If you suspect that the driver has not seen you, move out of the way. If a walker has a collision with an automobile, it does not matter who

Walk on the side of the road facing traffic.

Let cyclists have the right of way.

was right and who was wrong; the walker is the loser. Walk on the side of the road facing the oncoming traffic, and walk defensively. Make it impossible for a car to hit you.

## BICYCLES

Bicycle riders are supposed to obey all traffic laws; however, if you find yourself on a collision course with a bicycle, it is generally easier for you to move out of the way than it is for the person on the bicycle. Walk defensively. Don't allow a bicycle to hit you.

## DOGS

No dog should have the right to decide where or when you can walk on public property. There are no guarantees that dogs will not approach you, and you have to make your own decision about what to do. Following are some ideas that have worked for others and may work for you.

If a dog bothers you, decide what course of action is safest. It is best to avoid aggressive dogs.

If a dog comes at you, do not run away. You cannot run faster than a dog; running encourages a dog to continue the chase, and you leave yourself defenseless by turning your back toward the dog. Watch the dog but try to avoid eye contact; staring is a challenge. Do not be intimidated and do not panic. Decide what course of action is best for you. You may choose to back away slowly, but keep watching the dog. You may choose to walk on by slowly, or to pick up something to defend yourself, but keep watching the dog.

As a preventive measure, you might want to carry something with you when you walk, such as a protective spray or a walking stick. For a protective spray, water works fine for most dogs. For a determined and aggressive dog, cayenne pepper dissolved in water will usually work. One idea for a walking stick is the shaft of an old golf club with the head removed. It is lightweight, sturdy, and long enough to keep dogs away.

Check the route you want to walk in a car before you walk it the first time. Walk in a group or carry some protection the first time you walk a new course. If there is an area where you want to walk and dogs are running loose, talk politely with the owners about tying them up or fencing them in during that time. Most communities have a law against dogs running loose. If the owners are not cooperative, call the dog catcher or the police. Do not give a dog the right to limit your use of public property.

If you walk at night, wear a reflective vest or tape.

## LISTENING TO MUSIC

Listening to lively music while you fitness walk can energize your workout. However for safety purposes, it is best not to listen to music while you walk. Concentrating on it may distract you from walking safely and the volume may prevent you from hearing traffic. If you need to listen to music, keep the volume down and watch for traffic.

## NIGHT WALKING

It is safer to walk during the daylight hours than at night; however, it is not possible for everyone to walk during the daytime, especially during winter months, when there are fewer daylight hours. If you must walk when it is dark, consider the following safety suggestions.

1. Wear light-colored clothing, a reflective vest, or reflective tape on your clothing.
2. Stay away from dark streets and alleys.
3. Walk with another person or a group.
4. Let someone know your exact route and what time you expect to be back.
5. Wear identification, including who should be called in case of an emergency and any medical conditions you have that might need to be known for proper emergency medical treatment.

## WALKING SURFACES

Footing is an important consideration for fitness walkers. If you are unsure of a walking surface, slow down and stay alert for dangerous spots.

When walking on pavement, watch for holes and uneven cracks that might cause you to trip. On grass, gravel, or dirt roads, watch for bumps, holes, and sudden differences in firmness. If you are walking indoors on a smooth surface, such as wood, be cautious of any wet spots; they can be extremely slippery. If you are walking on a wet or icy surface, shorten your stride, keep your knees slightly bent, and use wider than normal foot placement.

Be especially cautious on potentially dangerous walking surfaces.

Repeated walking on hard surfaces may lead to shin splints and joint wear and tear. Consider alternating walking with biking and swimming.

## OVERTRAINING

It is possible to get too much exercise, called **overtraining.** Exercise is a physical stressor that stimulates positive changes to take place in your body. If you exercise too much or too often, however, your body may not be able to recover. This can lead to muscle soreness, injury, illnesses, and burnout. Adequate rest and proper nutrition are essential for recovery from exercise and improvement of physical fitness.

The following are some symptoms of overtraining:

- sudden, unexpected weight loss;
- depression;
- insomnia;
- increased resting heart rate;
- decreased work capacity;
- poor performance;
- loss of enjoyment;
- loss of motivation;

- frequent illness; and
- muscle, bone, and joint injuries.

If you have been training harder and longer than usual and you have several of these symptoms, it is possible that you are overtraining. Try to get more rest between exercise sessions, watch your nutritional intake more closely, and reduce the intensity, duration, or frequency of your exercise. If the problem is overtraining, you should start to feel better within a week or two.

Each individual has a rate at which he or she can best adapt to exercise. This is not a constant rate but one that changes continually and is influenced by the other stressors in life. Although there are general guidelines for exercise, you need to listen carefully to your body to find the right amount for you.

## FOOT CARE

The following tips will help you care for your feet.

1. Wear comfortable socks and good-quality shoes that fit properly.
2. Pay close attention to hot spots on your feet. Hot spots are the first stage of a blister.
3. Keep your feet clean and dry.
4. Keep your toenails trimmed properly.
5. If you have a foot problem, go to a podiatrist.

## FITNESS WALKING WITH WEIGHTS

Some fitness walkers use weights to increase the intensity of their workout. They generally add a weight vest, ankle weights, wrist weights, or hand weights. Although this may not be a problem for the advanced fitness walker, it can be dangerous for the beginner. The additional weight can interfere with the natural walking rhythm, cause unnecessary muscle soreness, and can produce an exercise load that is too great for an untrained heart. Other cautions include joint wear and tear and negative effects on posture.

## AIR POLLUTION

Air pollution can be a serious health problem and exercise hazard. Try to do your fitness walking in an area that has clean air. Air pollution can irritate your lungs and aggravate respiratory conditions such as asthma and bronchitis.

# NOISE POLLUTION

Noise pollution may cause additional stress, negating the psychological benefits of fitness walking. Avoid heavy construction sites, congested streets, and large airports. Plan to walk in parks, on running tracks, in quiet neighborhoods, on country roads, or in other quiet places.

## SUMMARY

- To be a safe fitness walker, there are special considerations that deserve attention.
- It's always a good idea to receive medical clearance from your physician before starting your fitness walking program.
- To avoid unnecessary pain and injury when starting your fitness walking program, start slowly and progress gradually.
- The dangers of heat-related problems including heat cramps, heat exhaustion, and heat stroke should be taken seriously.
- Drink plenty of fluid before, during, and after exercise, especially during hot, humid, and cold weather.
- Wear layers of clothing for cold-weather walking.
- Recreational drugs such as marijuana or crack cocaine have no place in an active, healthy lifestyle.
- Make it impossible for a car to hit you.
- A protective spray or walking stick can serve as preventive measures for dogs.
- For safety purposes, it is best not to listen to music while fitness walking.
- One important strategy for walking safely at night is to walk with others and wear reflective or light-colored clothing.
- Be cautious of walking surfaces, walking weights, pollution, and overtraining.
- Important tips for foot care include wearing comfortable socks and wearing good-quality shoes that fit.

# Assessment 4-1

## Determining Readiness for Fitness Walking

Name      Section   Date

Are you physically ready to participate in a fitness walking program? Answer each of the following questions by checking "Yes" or "No."

|  |  | Yes | No |
|---|---|---|---|
| 1. | Are you over 35 years of age? | ☐ | ☐ |
| 2. | Do you have any type of cardiovascular disease? | ☐ | ☐ |
| 3. | Do you have high blood pressure? | ☐ | ☐ |
| 4. | Do you ever experience chest pain? | ☐ | ☐ |
| 5. | Do you ever experience breathlessness? | ☐ | ☐ |
| 6. | Do you have any bone or joint problems? | ☐ | ☐ |
| 7. | Do you ever feel faint or dizzy? | ☐ | ☐ |
| 8. | Are you a smoker? | ☐ | ☐ |
| 9. | Have you been physically inactive for the past two years? | ☐ | ☐ |
| 10. | Do you have a weight problem? | ☐ | ☐ |
| 11. | Do you have any medical condition that could be a problem if you started walking? | ☐ | ☐ |

If you responded "Yes" to any of the questions, or if you have any doubt about your health, get medical clearance from your physician before starting a fitness walking program.

---

1. Which questions, if any, did you answer "Yes"? _____

2. If you did answer "Yes" to any of the questions, do you have medical clearance from your physician?

   Yes  No
   ☐   ☐

3. If you have any health problems, have you notified your instructor?

   Yes  No
   ☐   ☐

# CHAPTER 5

# WARM-UP, **COOL-DOWN,** AND FLEXIBILITY

## OBJECTIVES

*After reading this chapter, you should be able to do the following:*

- Explain why you should warm-up before your walking workout.
- Describe exactly how you should warm-up before your walking workout.
- Explain why you should cool-down after the aerobic portion of your walking workout.
- Describe exactly how you should cool-down after the aerobic portion of your walking workout.
- Define flexibility.
- List the general guidelines for stretching to increase flexibility.
- Demonstrate the four standing stretches recommended for fitness walking.

## KEY TERMS

*While reading this chapter, you will become familiar with the following terms:*

- ► Cool-Down
- ► Flexibility
- ► Static Stretch
- ► Stretching
- ► Warm-Up

# Fitness Tip

### How to Warm-Up

To warm-up, start each walk slowly. Gradually increase your walking speed as your body warms up.

## WARM-UP

A good **warm-up** before fitness walking can improve your performance and reduce your risk of injury. A proper warm-up for fitness walking requires five to ten minutes and should include slow walking and gentle stretching.

The walking portion of your warm-up should start slowly and gradually increase in speed. Your walking motion will become smoother and easier as your muscles and joints respond to the warm-up.

Stretching during the warm-up portion of your workout should be done gently and carefully. Vigorous stretching of cold muscles can result in injury and muscle soreness.

Warm-up exercises increase muscle temperature and allow your heart rate to increase gradually to your exercise heart rate. This is a safety measure to avoid unnecessary cardiac strain.

Walk slowly for three to five minutes to warm the muscles and joints before stretching. Gradually warm up before performing vigorous physical activity.

Stretching is a component of warming-up.

The warm-up period is also a time to get your mind ready for exercise. It is a time to focus your attention on your workout and on the development of your body. It is a time to think about your exercise goals and what you need to do during this exercise session to help you reach those goals. Exercise is more enjoyable and more effective if you have the proper mental attitude for your training session. While you are warming up, think positive thoughts about your workout and rededicate yourself to your exercise goals.

## Fitness Tip

### How to Cool Down

To cool-down, gradually slow your walking speed as you near the end of your walk, or walk for a few minutes at a slower pace after the aerobic portion of your walk.

A good warm-up should prepare you physically and mentally for the aerobic portion of your workout.

## COOL-DOWN

The **cool-down** is often the most neglected portion of a workout. Many exercisers skip this part of the exercise session, thinking that the important part of the workout is finished and that the cool-down doesn't really matter. Nothing could be farther from the truth.

In aviation, approximately 98 percent of accidents occur during takeoff or landing. In general, the same is true of exercise. The time of greatest risk is usually during the transition from rest to exercise and from exercise to rest.

▶ **Cool-Down**
Exercise movements designed to gradually reduce the intensity of activity and help your body make a smooth and safe transition from a high level of activity back toward a lower level of activity.

▶ **Flexibility**
The amount of movement, or range of motion, you have at each joint.

▶ **Static Stretch**
A type of stretching in which you hold the stretched position.

▶ **Stretching**
A type of exercise designed to increase or maintain your flexibility.

▶ **Warm-Up**
Exercise movements designed to gradually prepare your body for more vigorous activity.

Your cool-down should generally last at least five to ten minutes and include slow walking and stretching. The more vigorous the exercise or the less fit you are, the longer it takes to cool down safely.

During the walking portion of your cool-down, there should be a gradual reduction in your speed. This will result in a gradual reduction in oxygen demand, which will allow your heart to return slowly toward its resting rate.

The rhythmic contractions of your skeletal muscles help your heart maintain adequate circulation during exercise. As your skeletal muscles contract rhythmically during walking, your veins are alternately squeezed and released. This milking action forces the blood in your veins to move toward your heart. Rhythmic skeletal muscle contractions provide as much as 30 percent of the force necessary to circulate your blood during vigorous physical activity. If you stop and stand still after vigorous walking, the important rhythmic muscle contractions stop. Blood tends to accumulate in your veins, especially in your legs. Suddenly your heart must supply 100 percent of the force necessary for blood circulation because your skeletal muscles are no longer helping. This is an abrupt increase in workload for your heart. You might begin to feel "light-headed" or "dizzy," like you might faint. This is a dangerous time. However, it is easy to avoid this dangerous situation. Continue walking for a few minutes after the aerobic portion of your workout while gradually reducing your walking speed.

## FLEXIBILITY

**Flexibility** is the amount of movement, or range of motion, you have at each joint. Limited range of motion of a joint can limit performance in some activities and increase the risk of injury to the body's soft tissues (muscles, tendons, and ligaments). Thus, increased flexibility is a healthy goal for most people. **Stretching** to improve flexibility is best done after the aerobic portion of your workout, when the soft tissues and joints are warm.

### ▶ General Tips for Stretching to Increase Flexibility

1. Use **static stretch.** To perform a static stretch, move a joint to the limit of its normal range of motion. Then, gently apply pressure to move the joint slightly beyond the point where it normally stops. Hold this position. Do not bounce. Static stretch (stretch and hold) is recommended for the following reasons: (1) it is an effective method of increasing flexibility, (2) there is less risk of injury (when compared to a "bounce type" stretch) to the soft tissues being stretched, (3) it helps prevent or relieve muscle soreness, (4) it is easy to learn, and (5) it can be done without a partner.
2. Stretch to the point where you feel a sensation of tightness. You should be able to feel which muscle, or group of muscles, is being stretched, but it should not be painful. Hold this position.

3. Hold each static stretch for 10 to 30 seconds. Perform each stretch one, two, or three times.

4. Do not injure the soft tissues. You should not experience extreme discomfort or pain while stretching. If you experience extreme pain, you are stretching too far.

5. Breathe slowly, rhythmically, and comfortably while stretching. Do not hold your breath. If you cannot breathe normally while stretching, you are probably stretching too far.

## Fitness Tip

### Doing Standard Stretching Exercises

Perform the four standing stretch exercises gently before each walk to improve your performance and reduce your risk of injury. Do these stretches after each walk to improve your flexibility.

6. Stretch any time you feel tightness. Stretching does not have to be restricted to your workout.

7. Warm-up stretches with cold muscles and joints should be light and easy.

8. Be sure your muscles are completely warmed up before performing stretching exercises to increase flexibility. Walk for a few minutes after you have completed the aerobic portion of your workout to allow your heart rate to return toward a resting level. Then stretch your muscles. They will stay warm for a long time after exercise.

9. Make stretching a relaxing daily habit. Some people like to stretch when they get up in the morning. It makes them feel better. Some people like to stretch before going to bed. It helps them relax and sleep well. Some people stretch before and after their daily exercise. It improves their performance and reduces their risk of injury.

## ▶ Four Standing Stretches for Fitness Walking

Many fitness walkers do not stretch before and after walking. They say it takes too long, they don't feel like they have an appropriate place to stretch, and they don't want to sit down or lay down or get dirty. One solution is to combine stretching exercises and do them from a standing position.

The lunge and shoulder stretch.

## ▶ Stretch Number One—Lunge and Shoulder Stretch

- Head and trunk erect
- One leg back
- Back foot pointing straight ahead, heel on ground
- Top of hips tilted back, low back flat
- Back knee straight 15 seconds, bent 15 seconds
- Front knee bent
- Hands behind back, fingers interlaced
- Elbows as straight as possible
- Arms raised as high as possible
- Hold 10 to 30 seconds
- Change legs and hold 10 to 30 seconds
- Feel the stretch in the ankle of your back foot, back of your lower leg, front of your hip joint, front of your shoulder joint, and chest

The adductor, trunk, shoulder, and neck stretch.

## ▶ Stretch Number Two—Adductor, Trunk, Shoulder, and Neck Stretch

- Feet wide apart (2 to 3 times shoulder width)
- Hands together overhead, palms facing up
- Bend your right knee
- Lean toward your left
- Feel stretch in your left adductor, right side of trunk, right shoulder, and right side of neck
- Hold 10 to 30 seconds
- Change sides, bend your left knee and lean toward your right side
- Hold 10 to 30 seconds

The standing quadricep and shin stretch.

### ▶ Stretch Number Three—Standing Quadricep and Shin Stretch

- Bend your right knee
- Hold the *toes* of your right foot with your left hand
- Feel the stretch on the front of your lower leg (shin), front of your thigh, and front of your hip
- Hold 10 to 30 seconds
- Change sides, hold the toes of your left foot with your right hand
- Hold 10 to 30 seconds

Standing hamstring and low back stretch.

## ▶ Stretch Number Four—Standing Hamstring and Low Back Stretch

- Place the heel of your right foot on a step or bench (appropriate height for your flexibility)
- Place both hands on your right thigh above your knee
- Gently bend forward at your hip and waist with your right knee slightly bent
- Feel the gentle stretch in the back of your thigh (hamstrings) and your lower back
- Maintain a slight bend in your support leg
- Hold 10 to 30 seconds
- Change legs and hold 10 to 30 seconds

## SUMMARY

- Begin each walking session with a warm-up consisting of slow-to-moderate walking for three to five minutes followed by gentle stretching.
- Follow the more vigorous aerobic portion of your walking session with a cool-down consisting of moderate-to-slow walking for three to five minutes and stretching exercises to improve the flexibility of your primary walking muscles.
- Stretching to improve your flexibility should be done when your muscles and joints are thoroughly warmed up.
- Perform static stretching exercises to improve your flexibility.
- Perform the four standing stretches gently after your walking warm-up to improve your walking performance and reduce your risk of injury.
- Perform the four standing stretches after the aerobic portion of your walking session to increase the flexibility of your walking muscles.

# Assessment 5-1

Name                    Section        Date

The purpose of this assessment is for you to learn flexibility exercises that you can use as part of your fitness walking program. Perform each of the four fitness walking stretches in chapter 5. Follow the general tips for stretching in chapter 5. Answer the question following each stretch.

1. Perform standing stretch number one, the "Lunge and Shoulder Stretch." Did you feel the stretch in the ankle of your back foot, the back of your lower leg, the front of your hip joint, the front of your shoulder joints, and across your chest?

2. Perform standing stretch number two, the "Adductor, Trunk, Neck, and Shoulder Stretch." Did you feel the stretch in your shoulder, along the side of your trunk, along the side of your neck, and along the inside of your thigh?

3. Perform standing stretch number three, the "Standing Quadriceps and Shin Stretch." Did you feel the stretch along the front of your lower leg (shin), along the front of your thigh, and along the front of you hip?

4. Perform standing stretch number four, the "Standing Hamstring and Low Back Stretch." Did you feel the stretch along the back of your thigh (hamstrings) and along your lower back?

# CHAPTER 6

## FITNESS **WALKING**
### TEST

## OBJECTIVES

*After reading this chapter, you should be able to do the following:*

- Explain the benefits of testing your cardiovascular fitness.
- Discuss why the Rockport Fitness Walking Test is a good test of cardiovascular fitness for people who walk for fitness.
- Describe how to take the Rockport Fitness Walking Test.
- Understand how to find your fitness category from your test results.
- Recognize what your test results indicate.
- Determine when and why you should repeat the Rockport Fitness Walking Test.
- Demonstrate an understanding of how to use the fitness level charts in this chapter.
- Demonstrate your ability to count your heart rate.
- Demonstrate your ability to complete the Rockport Fitness Test and determine your current cardiovascular fitness level by yourself.

## KEY TERMS

*While reading this chapter, you will become familiar with the following terms:*

- ► Cardiovascular Fitness
- ► Carotid Artery
- ► Exercise Heart Rate
- ► Heart Rate

- ► Pulse
- ► Radial Artery
- ► Rockport Fitness Walking Test

## WHY TEST?

What is your present **cardiovascular fitness** level? This chapter will describe one walking test you can use to measure your cardiovascular fitness level.

Knowing your current fitness level can help you find a realistic place to start your fitness walking program. By starting at the appropriate exercise level, you will find that your walking program will be safer, more productive, and more enjoyable.

If you have been sedentary, be very cautious about taking any fitness test. Do not push yourself too hard during the test. It is much safer to complete the test comfortably and be classified in a lower fitness category than to push yourself too hard and risk injury. Some experts recommend beginning with a low-intensity starter program for at least two or three weeks before taking any fitness test.

Many people start exercise programs every year with unrealistic expectations. They start out highly motivated and full of enthusiasm, but with little knowledge of their present fitness level or of the amount of exercise they need. Consequently, they frequently start out doing too much. This often leads to muscle soreness, extreme fatigue, frustration, injury, or burnout. As a result, many of these people lose motivation and quit exercising.

It is unrealistic to think you can make up for years of bad habits in a few days. The benefits of regular exercise come from a lifetime habit of moderate exercise. It is better to start at a comfortable level of fitness walking and enjoy it for the rest of your life than to exercise at a high level for a few days and quit.

To prevent this from occurring, test yourself. This will enable you to start a fitness walking program that will best fit your needs and current physical condition. You will be able to enjoy your walking program while you progress gradually and safely.

Before taking the fitness walking tests, make sure it is medically safe for you to participate. Review the discussion of medical clearance in chapter 4 and complete Assessment 6-1 (at the end of this chapter) before taking the Rockport Fitness Walking Test.

## WHY THE ROCKPORT FITNESS WALKING TEST?

Researchers at the University of Massachusetts Medical School found that cardiovascular fitness can be estimated fairly accurately using four factors: age, gender, time to walk one mile, and heart rate at the completion of a one-mile walk. The researchers developed charts for estimating cardiovascular fitness level using these four factors and fitness norms from the American Heart Association. This field test of cardiovascular fitness is called the **Rockport Fitness Walking Test.**

# Fitness Tip

### Conducting the Rockport Fitness Walking Test

Learn how to conduct the Rockport Fitness Walking Test by yourself. This is an important first step in taking responsibility for your cardiovascular fitness.

## HOW TO TAKE THE ROCKPORT FITNESS WALKING TEST

To take the Rockport Fitness Walking Test, you need to be able to count your heart rate. Gently place the fingertips of your index finger and middle finger on the **radial artery.** You will find this artery on the palm side of your forearm, just above your wrist and on the thumb side of your forearm.

You can also count your pulse by placing the same two fingertips on the **carotid artery.** You will find this artery by placing your fingertips along the side of your trachea (windpipe) near the top.

▶ **Cardiovascular Fitness**
The ability of your heart, blood vessels, blood, and lungs to deliver oxygen to your cells, especially muscle cells during long-term physical activity.

▶ **Carotid Artery**
A blood vessel in the neck often used to count heart rate.

▶ **Exercise Heart Rate**
Heart rate during exercise. A very close approximation of your exercise heart rate can be determined by locating your pulse immediately after you stop exercising, within five seconds, and taking a heart rate count for a short time (15 seconds).

▶ **Heart Rate**
The rate at which your heart pumps blood. This is traditionally expressed in beats per minute.

▶ **Pulse**
The rhythmic expansion of the arteries caused by the contractions of the heart.

▶ **Radial Artery**
A blood vessel, near the wrist, often used to count heart rate.

▶ **Rockport Fitness Walking Test**
A test of cardiovascular fitness that uses walking as the activity.

To take the walking test, you need a watch or clock that can measure time in minutes and seconds. Find a flat, measured mile to walk. A quarter-mile track is an excellent place. If there is not a track available, measure a one-mile course where you can walk continuously. Avoid traffic and stoplights. It is a good idea to measure a half mile so you can walk out and back. That way, you will know when you are halfway through the test and you will end where you started.

Walk the mile as fast as you can while maintaining a constant pace. Running is not allowed. However, think safety first. Do not endanger your health. Slow down if the pace is too fast.

Two measurements are necessary to determine your current fitness level. One is the number of minutes and seconds it takes you to walk one mile. The other is your heart rate immediately after finishing the mile (table 6-1). Speeding up or slowing down near the end of the test will affect your heart rate, walking time, and test results. Maintain a steady pace.

**TABLE 6-1**

**Measuring Your Pulse**

| 15 Second Pulse Count | Beats Per Minute Heart Rate | | 15 Second Pulse Count | Beats Per Minute Heart Rate |
|:---:|:---:|:---:|:---:|:---:|
| 15 | 60 | _____ | 36 | 144 |
| 16 | 64 | _____ | 37 | 148 |
| 17 | 68 | _____ | 38 | 152 |
| 18 | 72 | _____ | 39 | 156 |
| 19 | 76 | _____ | 40 | 160 |
| 20 | 80 | _____ | 41 | 164 |
| 21 | 84 | _____ | 42 | 168 |
| 22 | 88 | _____ | 43 | 172 |
| 23 | 92 | _____ | 44 | 176 |
| 24 | 96 | _____ | 45 | 180 |
| 25 | 100 | _____ | 46 | 184 |
| 26 | 104 | _____ | 47 | 188 |
| 27 | 108 | _____ | 48 | 192 |
| 28 | 112 | _____ | 49 | 196 |
| 29 | 116 | _____ | 50 | 200 |
| 30 | 120 | _____ | 51 | 204 |
| 31 | 124 | _____ | 52 | 208 |
| 32 | 128 | _____ | 53 | 212 |
| 33 | 132 | _____ | 54 | 216 |
| 34 | 136 | _____ | 55 | 220 |
| 35 | 140 | _____ | | |

Use either the carotid artery or radial artery to count your pulse.

As soon as you cross the finish line record your time in minutes and seconds. Immediately, within five seconds after finish, locate your **pulse** and count the number of heart beats in 15 seconds. Multiply the number of heart beats in 15 seconds times four to get your **heart rate** in beats per minute.

The reason for locating your pulse immediately and taking a 15-second pulse count is to find your **exercise heart rate.** A great deal of recovery can occur within the first minute after you stop exercising; therefore, if you wait too long to locate your pulse, or take a longer count, you will not get your exercise heart rate and your test result will not be valid.

## HOW TO FIND YOUR FITNESS CATEGORY

Once your results are recorded you can determine your current fitness level by looking at the appropriate fitness level chart in this chapter for your age and gender.

On the horizontal line at the top of the chart, locate your time to complete the one-mile walk. Place a mark on the line at that point.

On the vertical line on the left side of the chart locate your exercise heart rate in beats per minute. Place a mark on the line at that point.

Draw a line straight down from your time and another line straight across from your heart rate. The point at which the two lines intersect indicates your cardiovascular fitness level.

The relative fitness charts for 20–29-year-olds can be used for individuals under the age of 20.

**AGE 20-29**

## MEN'S FITNESS LEVEL CHART

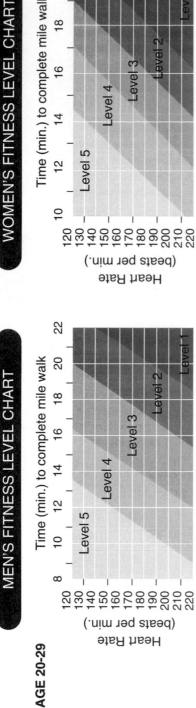

Time (min.) to complete mile walk

Heart Rate (beats per min.)

Level 5
Level 4
Level 3
Level 2
Level 1

## WOMEN'S FITNESS LEVEL CHART

Time (min.) to complete mile walk

Heart Rate (beats per min.)

Level 5
Level 4
Level 3
Level 2
Level 1

**AGE 30-39**

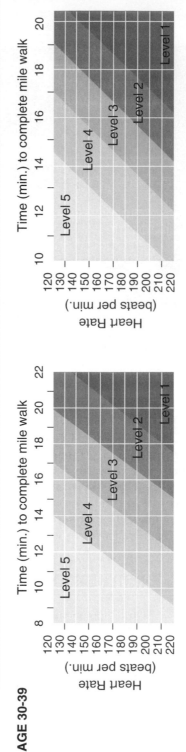

Time (min.) to complete mile walk

Heart Rate (beats per min.)

Level 5
Level 4
Level 3
Level 2
Level 1

Time (min.) to complete mile walk

Heart Rate (beats per min.)

Level 5
Level 4
Level 3
Level 2
Level 1

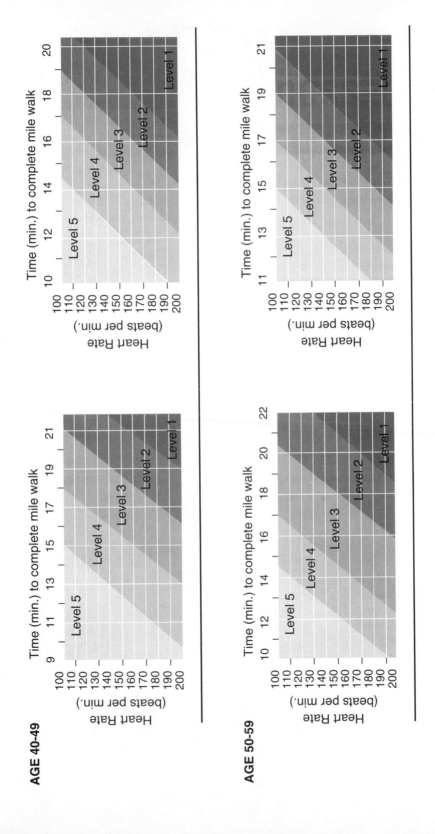

**AGE 40-49**

**AGE 50-59**

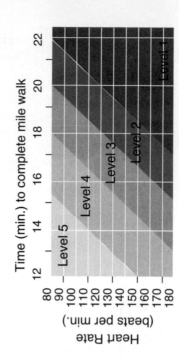

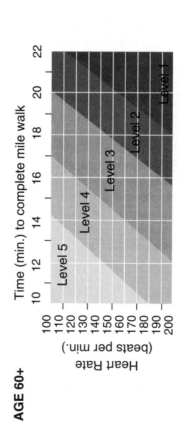

**AGE 60+**

## INTERPRETING THE RESULTS

What do your results mean? To understand your performance on the test, let's use as an example a 22-year-old woman who scored in the level 4 fitness category. Her results indicate that she is above average in cardiovascular fitness when compared to other women of her age group (20–29).

## RETESTING

How often should you retest yourself on the Rockport Fitness Walking Test? The scientists who developed the Rockport Fitness Walking Test, and the walking programs in the next chapter, recommend that you finish a 20-week walking program before taking the test again. However, many excellent educators who teach fitness walking recommend testing after four weeks or eight weeks or 15 weeks. When you retest you will probably find that your time to walk one mile is faster or your heart rate is lower, or both. Either of these is an indication that your cardiovascular fitness is better than it was the last time you completed the test.

When you retest after completing a 20-week fitness walking program, you may find that you have moved up to another fitness level. If that is the case, base your next fitness walking program on your new fitness level.

When you reach the point where you are satisfied with your cardiovascular fitness level, change to a maintenance walking program. Taking the walking test two or three times a year should be sufficient once you are on a maintenance program; however, some regular walkers prefer to take the test once a month. This helps them monitor their fitness level on a regular basis and provides motivation for them to keep up with their exercise program.

### SUMMARY

- Testing your cardiovascular fitness enables you to know your current fitness level, plan an exercise program that is appropriate and enjoyable for your fitness level, and measure your improvement.
- The Rockport Fitness Walking Test allows you to use the same activity for training and testing.
- To complete the Rockport Fitness Walking Test you need to walk one mile as quickly as possible while maintaining a steady, safe pace.
- At the end of your one mile walking test you need to record your walking time in minutes and seconds and your exercise heart rate in beats per minute.
- To determine your cardiovascular fitness category use the charts in this chapter.

- To use the fitness category charts in this chapter you need your age, gender, time to walk one mile, and exercise heart rate.
- Periodically repeating the Rockport Fitness Walking Test will enable you to know your current fitness level, plan an appropriate walking program, and measure your improvement.

# Assessment 6-1

Name _____  Section _____  Date _____

The purpose of this assessment is to learn how to count your pulse at the radial artery and the carotid artery.

You need to know how to count your pulse before taking the Rockport Fitness Walking Test. Read or review the section in chapter 6 that explains how to count your pulse to determine your heart rate.

Find your pulse within 5 seconds and count it for 15 seconds.

Practice three times using the radial artery and three times using the carotid artery.

To convert your pulse count to heart rate in beats per minute, multiply each 15-second count by four.

| **Radial** | **Carotid** |
|---|---|
| 1. 15 sec. count _____ × 4 = _____. | 1. 15 sec. count _____ × 4 = _____. |
| 2. 15 sec. count _____ × 4 = _____. | 2. 15 sec. count _____ × 4 = _____. |
| 3. 15 sec. count _____ × 4 = _____. | 3. 15 sec. count _____ × 4 = _____. |

Were you able to locate your pulse at the carotid artery and the radial artery? _____

Which artery was easier for you to locate and count your pulse? _____

Were your pulse counts fairly consistent for each artery? _____

Were your pulse counts fairly consistent comparing one artery to the other? _____

Which artery will you use at the end of your Rockport Fitness Walking Test? _____

# Assessment 6-2

## Rockport Fitness Walking Test

Name _____  Section _____  Date _____

The purpose of this assessment is to determine your current fitness level using the Rockport Fitness Walking Test. Read the medical and safety guidelines located in chapter 4 before taking the test.

Follow the directions for the Rockport Fitness Walking Test found in chapter 6. When you finish the Walking Test, record your results. Once your results are recorded, follow the directions in chapter 6 to find your fitness category.

Age _____ Gender _____

One-mile walk time in minutes and seconds _____

Exercise heart rate, 15 second count _____ × 4 = _____ BPM

Fitness level _____

Did you record your time in minutes and seconds immediately after finishing the one-mile walk? _____

Did you locate your pulse within 5 seconds and count your pulse for 15 seconds to get your exercise heart rate? _____

Were you able to find your fitness level using the charts in chapter 6? _____

# CHAPTER 7

## FITNESS **WALKING** PROGRAMS

---

## OBJECTIVES

*After reading this chapter, you should be able to do the following:*

- Locate the appropriate Rockport Fitness Walking Program for you based on the results of your Rockport Fitness Walking Test.
- Use the Rockport Program charts to explain how far (mileage), how hard (heart rate), and how often (times per week) you should walk during any given week of your walking program.
- Calculate 60, 70, and 80 percent of your age-predicted maximum heart rate (APMHR).
- Calculate your estimated maximum heart rate (EMHR).
- Explain why exercise heart rate is an indication of exercise intensity.
- Use the American Heart Association Program Chart to describe how long you should walk in your target heart rate zone for any given week of the program.
- Explain the meaning of the acronym FITT.
- Describe and explain the guidelines for fitness walking to develop cardiovascular fitness.
- Identify and explain the five components of health-related physical fitness.
- Recognize the best order of exercises to develop all components of health-related physical fitness in each workout.

## KEY TERMS

*While reading this chapter, you will become familiar with the following terms:*

- ► Age-Predicted Maximum Heart Rate (APMHR)
- ► Estimated Maximum Heart Rate (EMHR)
- ► Exercise Heart Rate

- ► FITT
- ► Frequency
- ► Intensity
- ► Time
- ► Type

Exercise is like medicine. To be beneficial you need the right type and the right amount. Fitness walking is the right type of exercise for most people. This chapter will help you select the right amount. In this chapter you will find three different ways to get started on a walking program:

1. Rockport programs
2. American Heart Association program
3. Information to design your own program

## ROCKPORT WALKING PROGRAMS

The first set of programs is The Rockport Fitness Walking Programs. If you have completed the Rockport Fitness Walking Test you are ready to select your fitness walking program. The Rockport Walking Programs (table 7-1) correspond to your cardiovascular fitness level as measured by the Rockport Fitness Walking Test.

The Rockport Walking Programs were developed by the cardiologists and exercise scientists at the University of Massachusetts Medical School. They are designed to improve or maintain your current level of fitness. For best results, follow the programs closely.

# Fitness Tip

## Selecting a Walking Program

Check your results from the Rockport Fitness Walking Test. Use this information to determine the Rockport Fitness Walking Program that is right for you.

At the end of each 20-week period, retake the Rockport Fitness Walking Test to determine your new fitness level and exercise program.

On each program, you will see columns labeled "Pace" and "Heart Rate." The pace listed is only an approximation. Walking speed should be the pace that keeps your heart rate at the appropriate percentage listed.

► **Age-Predicted Maximum Heart Rate (APMHR)**
See estimated Maximum Heart Rate (EMHR).

► **Estimated Maximum Heart Rate (EMHR)**
220 minus your age gives you a rough estimate of your maximum heart rate. There is a wide range of healthy normal maximum heart rates that are not average. Maximum heart rate is the fastest your heart can beat under the most strenuous conditions, it is NOT your exercise heart rate.

► **Exercise Heart Rate**
Your heart rate during exercise, which serves an indication of how hard you are working.

► **FITT**
Frequency, Intensity, Time, Type of exercise to produce the desired results.

► **Frequency**
How often (how many times per week) you need to exercise to produce the desired results.

► **Intensity**
How hard (heart rate) you need to exercise to produce the desired results.

► **Time**
How long (duration) each exercise session needs to be to produce the desired results.

► **Type**
The kind of exercise that needs to be done to produce the desired results.

# TABLE 7-1
## Rockport Walking Programs

### Level 1

| Week | 1–2 | 3–4 | 5 | 6 | 7–8 | 9 | 10 | 11 | 12–13 | 14 | 15–16 | 17–18 | 19–20 |
|---|---|---|---|---|---|---|---|---|---|---|---|---|---|
| Warm-Up / Cool-Down | 5–7 | 5–7 | 5–7 | 5–7 | 5–7 | 5–7 | 5–7 | 5–7 | 5–7 | 5–7 | 5–7 | 5–7 | 5–7 |
| Mileage | 1.0 | 1.25 | 1.5 | 1.5 | 1.75 | 2.0 | 2.0 | 2.0 | 2.25 | 2.5 | 2.5 | 2.75 | 3.0 |
| Pace (mph) | 3.0 | 3.0 | 3.0 | 3.5 | 3.5 | 3.5 | 3.75 | 3.75 | 3.75 | 3.75 | 4.0 | 4.0 | 4.0 |
| Heart Rate (% of max) | 60 | 60 | 60 | 60–70 | 60–70 | 60–70 | 60–70 | 70 | 70 | 70 | 70 | 70–80 | 70–80 |
| Frequency (times/week) | 5 | 5 | 5 | 5 | 5 | 5 | 5 | 5 | 5 | 5 | 5 | 5 | 5 |

### Level 2

| Week | 1–2 | 3–4 | 5–6 | 7 | 8–9 | 10–12 | 13 | 14 | 15–16 | 17–18 | 19–20 |
|---|---|---|---|---|---|---|---|---|---|---|---|
| Warm-Up / Cool-Down | 5–7 | 5–7 | 5–7 | 5–7 | 5–7 | 5–7 | 5–7 | 5–7 | 5–7 | 5–7 | 5–7 |
| Mileage | 1.5 | 1.75 | 2.0 | 2.0 | 2.25 | 2.5 | 2.75 | 2.75 | 3.0 | 3.25 | 3.5 |
| Pace (mph) | 3.0 | 3.0 | 3.0 | 3.5 | 3.5 | 3.5 | 3.5 | 4.0 | 4.0 | 4.0 | 4.0 |
| Heart Rate (% of max) | 60–70 | 60–70 | 60–70 | 70 | 70 | 70 | 70 | 70–80 | 70–80 | 70–80 | 70–80 |
| Frequency (times/week) | 5 | 5 | 5 | 5 | 5 | 5 | 5 | 5 | 5 | 5 | 5 |

### Level 3

| Week | 1 | 2 | 3–4 | 5 | 6–8 | 9–10 | 11–12 | 13–14 | 15 | 16–17 | 18–20 | maintenance |
|---|---|---|---|---|---|---|---|---|---|---|---|---|
| Warm-Up / Cool-Down | 5–7 | 5–7 | 5–7 | 5–7 | 5–7 | 5–7 | 5–7 | 5–7 | 5–7 | 5–7 | 5–7 | |
| Mileage | 2.0 | 2.25 | 2.5 | 2.75 | 2.75 | 3.0 | 3.0 | 3.25 | 3.5 | 3.5 | 4.0 | |
| Pace (mph) | 3.0 | 3.0 | 3.0 | 3.0 | 3.5 | 3.5 | 4.0 | 4.0 | 4.0 | 4.5 | 4.5 | |
| Heart Rate (% of max) | 70 | 70 | 70 | 70 | 70 | 70 | 70–80 | 70–80 | 70–80 | 70–80 | 70–80 | |
| Frequency (times/week) | 5 | 5 | 5 | 5 | 5 | 5 | 5 | 5 | 5 | 5 | 3–5 | |

**Level 4**

| Week | 1 | 2 | 3–4 | 5 | 6 | 7 | 8 | 9–10 | 11–14 | 15–20 | maintenance |
|---|---|---|---|---|---|---|---|---|---|---|---|
| Warm-Up / Cool-Down | 5–7 | 5–7 | 5–7 | 5–7 | 5–7 | 5–7 | 5–7 | 5–7 | 5–7 | 5–7 | 5–7 |
| Mileage | 2.5 | 2.75 | 3.0 | 3.25 | 3.5 | 3.5 | 3.75 | 4.0 | 4.0 | 4.0 | 4.0 |
| Pace (mph) | 3.5 | 3.5 | 3.5 | 3.5 | 3.5 | 4.0 | 4.0 | 4.0 | 4.5 | 4.5 | 4.5 |
| Heart Rate (% of max) | 70 | 70 | 70 | 70 | 70–80 | 70–80 | 70–80 | 70–80 | 70–80 | 70–80 | 70–80 |
| Frequency (times/week) | 5 | 5 | 5 | 5 | 5 | 5 | 5 | 5 | 5 | 5 | 3–5 |

**Level 5**

| Week | 1 | 2 | 3 | 4 | 5 | 6 | 7–20 | maintenance |
|---|---|---|---|---|---|---|---|---|
| Warm-Up / Cool-Down | 5–7 | 5–7 | 5–7 | 5–7 | 5–7 | 5–7 | 5–7 | 5–7 |
| Mileage | 3.0 | 3.25 | 3.5 | 3.5 | 3.75 | 4.0 | 4.0 | 4.0 |
| Pace (mph) | 4.0 | 4.0 | 4.0 | 4.5 | 4.5 | 4.5 | 4.5 | 4.5 |
| Heart Rate (% of max) | 70 | 70 | 70 | 70–80 | 70–80 | 70–80 | 70–80 | 70–80 |
| Frequency (times/week) | 5 | 5 | 5 | 5 | 5 | 5 | 5 | 3–5 |

# AMERICAN HEART ASSOCIATION WALKING PROGRAM

The second program is The American Heart Association Walking Program (table 7-2), which is safe for most beginners. Each workout should consist of a warm-up, a walk within your target heart rate zone, and a cool-down. Your target heart rate zone for this program is an exercise heart rate that is between 60 percent and 75 percent of your maximum heart rate. With this walking program you should walk at least three times each week.

**TABLE 7-2**
**American Heart Association Walking Program**

| Week | Target Zone Exercising | Total Time in Minutes (warm-up + target zone exercising + cool-down) |
|---|---|---|
| 1 | Walk briskly 5 min. | 15 min. |
| 2 | Walk briskly 7 min. | 17 min. |
| 3 | Walk briskly 9 min. | 19 min. |
| 4 | Walk briskly 11 min. | 21 min. |
| 5 | Walk briskly 13 min. | 23 min. |
| 6 | Walk briskly 15 min. | 25 min. |
| 7 | Walk briskly 18 min. | 28 min. |
| 8 | Walk briskly 20 min. | 30 min. |
| 9 | Walk briskly 23 min. | 33 min. |
| 10 | Walk briskly 26 min. | 36 min. |
| 11 | Walk briskly 28 min. | 38 min. |
| 12 | Walk briskly 30 min. | 40 min. |
| 13 on: | Check your pulse periodically to see if you are exercising within your target zone. As you get more in shape, try exercising within the upper range of your target heart zone. Remember that your goal is to continue getting the benefits you seek while enjoying your activity. | |

Reproduced with permission. WALKING FOR A HEALTHY HEART, American Heart Association.

# Fitness Tip

## Designing Your Walking Program

Design your fitness walking program using the following guidelines:

Frequency—three to seven days per week

Intensity—60 to 80 percent of your maximum heart rate

Time—20 to 60 minutes

## GUIDELINES FOR PLANNING YOUR OWN FITNESS WALKING PROGRAM

The third way to get started on a fitness walking program is to plan your own program. The Rockport Fitness Walking Programs and The American Heart Association Program are excellent; however, some walkers may want to plan their own fitness walking program. The following guidelines will help you plan your own program.

## THE RIGHT AMOUNT OF EXERCISE

The right amount of exercise is determined by the characteristics of FITT—**frequency, intensity, time,** and **type.**

### ▶ Frequency

How often should you walk? Fitness walking must be performed regularly to be effective. The recommended frequency for fitness walking is three to seven days per week.

### ▶ Intensity

How fast do you need to walk? Intensity refers to how hard you need to exercise to benefit from each training session. **Exercise heart rate** provides an indication of how hard you are exercising. A guideline for fitness walking is to reach an exercise heart rate between 60 and 80 percent of your maximum heart rate. To estimate your maximum heart rate, subtract your age from 220.

Healthy beginning fitness walkers should start out at a low intensity, 60 to 70 percent of their maximum heart rate. Some beginners may need to start at 50 percent of their estimated maximum heart rate. Advanced fitness walkers may choose to exercise at a higher intensity—80 to 90 percent of their maximum heart rate.

Some people believe the old athletic myth of "no pain, no gain." It is not true. They believe you must exercise until you are in pain for exercise to be beneficial. This is one of the reasons they do not exercise regularly.

▶ **Time**

How long do you need to walk? You should walk for 20 to 60 minutes at your prescribed exercise heart rate. If you are just starting a fitness walking program, keep the intensity low and the duration short. Gradually increase the duration first, then the intensity.

▶ **Type**

Why is fitness walking the right type of exercise? Fitness walking is considered the right type of exercise because it is aerobic. Aerobic exercises develop cardiovascular fitness, reduce cardiovascular disease, and help lower body fat. These benefits are a result of using large muscle groups rhythmically and continuously. This causes the body to use larger amounts of oxygen and calories for an extended time.

## Guidelines for Fitness Walking to Develop Cardiovascular Fitness

| FITT | |
|------|------|
| Frequency | Three to seven days per week |
| Intensity | 60 to 80 percent of maximum heart rate |
| Time | 20 to 60 minutes |
| Type | Aerobic exercise (fitness walking) |

## RECOVERY

How much exercise is too much? As a guideline, if you experience extreme muscle soreness the next day and cannot repeat your fitness walking workout, you have done too much and need to reduce the amount of exercise the next time.

Exercise is only the stimulus for positive biological changes to occur in your body. These changes occur during the recovery time between exercise sessions. Make sure the exercise stimulus is not too severe and that you get adequate rest and nutrition between walking workouts.

A problem for some middle-aged people is that they want to get back into the physical condition they were in when they were young. This is not a realistic expectation. Many people who have been inactive for a long time want to get in shape quickly; however, biological adaptation is a relatively slow process. You cannot expect to reverse the effects of years of sedentary living in a few days or weeks. These people often fall into the trap of thinking that, if a little exercise is good, then more must be better. This is only true to a point. Beyond that point, additional exercise can be harmful. Follow the exercise guidelines. Progress slowly and safely. If you try to progress too quickly, you are likely to become injured. When you are injured, you are likely to lose your motivation to exercise. If you lose your motivation and quit, you will not achieve the benefits that come from regular exercise.

If you are exercising for your health, you do not need to improve forever. When you reach the fitness level you want, change to a walking program that will keep you at that level.

These guidelines will help you select and maintain a safe and enjoyable walking program that you can stay with and benefit from for the rest of your life.

Because there is less to keep track of, some people prefer creating their own program rather than using the Rockport program. If you follow these guidelines, all you need to keep track of is your total minutes walked at your exercise heart rate. This method also gives you greater freedom to walk new courses, because you do not need to know the exact distance, only walking time and heart rate.

## TOTAL HEALTH-RELATED PHYSICAL FITNESS

Walking is an excellent exercise but it does not develop all aspects of health-related physical fitness. Total health-related physical fitness includes cardiovascular endurance, body composition, strength, muscular endurance, and flexibility.

### ▶ Cardiovascular Endurance

Cardiovascular endurance refers to your ability to continue vigorous total body activity for a relatively long period. As mentioned previously, to develop cardiovascular endurance, you should perform exercises that use large muscle groups rhythmically and continuously. Maintain an exercise heart rate that is 60 to 80 percent of your maximum heart rate for 20 to 60 minutes, and repeat this workout three to seven times each week.

### ▶ Body Composition

Body composition refers to the amount of muscle, fat, bone, and other tissues that makeup the body. The best exercises to achieve and maintain healthy levels of body fat are those that use large muscle groups rhythmically and continuously. Exercise at a heart rate that is 60 to 80 percent of your estimated maximum heart rate for 30 to 60 minutes and repeat this workout five to seven days per week.

### ▶ Strength

Strength refers to the amount of force a muscle can exert. To develop strength, perform exercises that involve movement through a full range of motion against resistance. Use a resistance that is 70 to 100 percent of your maximum voluntary contraction (the most weight you can lift one time) and execute 1 to 10 repeti-

Total fitness includes cardiovascular endurance, body composition, strength, muscular endurance, and flexibility.

tions. Perform each exercise for one to three sets and repeat your strength training program three days per week. There are entire books devoted to strength and muscle endurance training. It is not within the scope of this book to adequately describe strength training principles and programs.

## ▶ Muscle Endurance

Muscle endurance refers to the ability of individual muscles or muscle groups to exert force for many repetitions or to hold a position for an extended time. To develop muscle endurance, perform exercises that require movement through a full range of motion against resistance. Use a resistance that is 50 to 70 percent of your maximum voluntary contraction (the heaviest you can lift one time) and execute 20 to 30 repetitions. Perform one to three sets of each exercise and repeat your muscle endurance exercises three to five days per week.

## ▶ Flexibility

To develop flexibility, use static stretch exercises. Stretch to the point where you feel a sensation of tightness, and hold each stretch for 15 to 30 seconds. Perform each stretch one to three times, and repeat your stretching program three to seven days per week.

## A TOTAL HEALTH-RELATED PHYSICAL FITNESS PROGRAM

Fitness walking programs, including the stretching exercises during the warm-up and cool-down, develop cardiovascular endurance, muscular endurance, flexibility, and a healthy body fat level. Adding a few strength exercises after the walking portion, and before the stretching portion of your cool-down, results in a good total health-related physical fitness program.

A total health-related physical fitness program is as follows:

- Warm-up walking
- Gentle stretch
- Fitness walking at exercise heart rate
- Cool-down walking
- Strength and muscle endurance exercises
- Cool-down stretching (flexibility stretching)

## SUMMARY

- This chapter has described three different ways to plan your fitness walking program.
  1) Use the Rockport Fitness Walking Programs.
  2) Use the American Heart Association Walking Program.
  3) Design your own walking program based on the exercise guidelines in this chapter.
- The Rockport Walking Programs are each 20 weeks long and are based on your results from the Rockport Fitness Walking Test.
- The American Heart Association Walking Program is a 12-week starter program. After completing the 12-week starter program you should continue with a maintenance program of 30 minutes of brisk walking at least three times each week.
- If you choose to design your own walking program you will need to walk 20 to 60 minutes at a heart rate that is 60 to 80 percent of your maximum heart rate, and three to seven days per week. Start by walking for a shorter time, at a lower heart rate, and fewer days per week. First increase the time per walk, then the number of days per week, and last the heart rate.
- Adequate rest and nutrition are critical to your progress.
- Walking is an excellent exercise but it does not develop all components of health-related physical fitness.
- The components of health-related physical fitness are:
  1) Cardiovascular Endurance
  2) Body Composition
  3) Strength
  4) Muscular Endurance
  5) Flexibility

## A TOTAL HEALTH-RELATED PHYSICAL FITNESS PROGRAM

# Assessment 7-1

Name                                    Section                Date

The purpose of this assessment is to determine your exercise heart rate range. This will help you monitor your exercise intensity.

Your **age-predicted maximum heart rate (APMHR)** is determined by subtracting your age from 220. This is your **estimated maximum heart rate (EHMR)** based on your age.

Multiply your estimated maximum heart rate by .60 to find 60 percent of that rate.

Multiply your estimated maximum heart rate by .80 to find 80 percent of that rate.

| Example | | | Step 1 | | |
|---|---|---|---|---|---|
| 220 | | | | 220 | |
| − 20 | age | | | − _____ | your age |
| = 200 | EMHR | | | = | EMHR |
| | | | Step 2 | | |
| 200 | EMHR | | | _____ | your EMHR |
| × .60 | | | | × .60 | |
| = 120 | lower limit | | | = | lower limit |
| | | | Step 3 | | |
| 200 | EMHR | | | _____ | your EMHR |
| × .80 | | | | × .80 | |
| = 160 | upper limit | | | = | upper limit |

| Example exercise heart rate range | Your exercise heart rate range |
|---|---|
| lower limit ___120___ | lower limit _____ |
| upper limit ___160___ | upper limit _____ |

# CHAPTER 8

## FITNESS WALKING TECHNIQUES

## OBJECTIVES

*After reading this chapter, you should be able to do the following:*

* Apply specific walking techniques to improve your speed, stride length, and efficiency.
* Describe other strategies to increase your workout intensity.
* Understand the demands of high-intensity workouts.

## KEY TERMS

*While reading this chapter, you will become familiar with the following terms:*

► Brisk Pace
► Efficiency
► Horizontal Energy

► Speed
► Stride Length
► Vertical Energy

# Fitness Tip

## Focusing on Each Technique

Learn one technique at a time, focusing on one each workout. After practicing each technique until it becomes natural, combine them to become a highly skilled fitness walker.

Remember the last time you were late and you walked at a quickened pace? Chances are, you used several of the techniques that will be highlighted in this chapter.

To receive optimum benefits from fitness walking, it is necessary to walk at a **brisk pace.** Adopting specific techniques for fitness walking will increase your **speed, stride length,** and **efficiency.** As you acquire new skills, you should also improve your balance, coordination, body control, and agility.

Once you apply the fitness walking techniques, your pace will become faster. Your heart and lungs will work harder to supply the oxygen needed to the working muscles. This will improve your cardiovascular conditioning.

## TECHNIQUE 1: POSTURE AND ALIGNMENT

For the smoothest walking motion, maintain correct posture and body alignment. Apply the guidelines in Assessment 8-1 while you walk.

Technique 1:
Posture and alignment.

## TECHNIQUE 2: HEEL CONTACT

From a position of correct posture, swing one leg forward. Land on your heel. Do not land flat-footed or on the ball of your foot. (See Assessment 8-2.)

## TECHNIQUE 3: HEEL-TO-TOE ROLL

Once your heel makes contact with the ground, begin to roll your foot forward, keeping your weight slightly toward the outer edge of your foot until reaching your toes. Your foot acts as a natural rocker bottom for continuous forward motion. As you roll your foot forward with your weight toward the outer edge, keep your knees pointing straight ahead. (See Assessment 8-3.)

## TECHNIQUE 4: PUSH-OFF

Following the heel-to-toe roll, continue your forward motion with a push-off from your toes. Resist the temptation to

Technique 2: Heel contact.

▶ **Brisk Pace**
Fitness walking performed at a speed that produces desirable health benefits.

▶ **Efficiency**
To walk with a minimum of effort.

▶ **Horizontal Energy**
Walking performed with a minimum of up-and-down movement.

▶ **Speed**
The rate at which walking is performed.

▶ **Stride Length**
The distance covered as measured from the toes of the back foot to the heel of the front foot.

▶ **Vertical Energy**
A type of up and down movement that wastes useful energy for walking.

Technique 3: Heel-to-toe roll.

# Fitness Tip

## Evaluating Your Walking Form

Have your instructor or someone else videotape your fitness walking form. This can help you evaluate your skills and determine how close you are to the recommended techniques.

Techniques 4 and 5: Push-off and arm swing.

pick up your foot early, as you might do in casual walking. Keep your foot in contact with the ground as long as possible. You can lengthen your stride on each step by pushing off with your toes.

To reduce excessive side-to-side swaying and undue stress on your joints, keep your support foot pointing straight ahead. If your body rises and falls with each step, you may be pushing off from the front part of your foot instead of your toes. If this happens, reduce your speed and focus on the push-off.

Stretching exercises are recommended before you walk to improve your ankle, foot, and toe flexibility for a greater range of motion on the push-off. (See Assessment 8-4.)

## TECHNIQUE 5: ARM SWING

The arms play an important role in fitness walking. Your arms and legs are like teammates—the faster you move your legs, the faster your arms must swing to counterbalance.

To increase your walking speed, bend your arms to about a 90° angle at the elbow joint. Your hands should be in a relaxed fist position, with your palms facing inward. In this position, your arms should swing naturally forward and backward from the shoulder joint. Each arm should swing in a natural path and remain fairly close to your body to avoid side-to-side swaying of your upper body. On the forward swing, your hand should rise to the level of the xiphoid process at the bottom of the sternum (where the ribs join at the bottom of the chest). On the backswing your hand should stop at the waist/hip area. (See Assessment 8-5.)

## TECHNIQUE 6: HIP MOVEMENT

Keep your back foot in contact with the ground until you have full extension of your leg and you push off from your toes. When swinging your leg to the front, reach forward with your front foot as far as comfort will allow. This technique can add as much as eight inches to your stride length.

Using the hips more reduces the amount of up-and-down movement with each step, converting wasted **vertical energy** into useful **horizontal energy**. Also, the abdominal and hip muscles are exercised more vigorously with increased hip movement.

This hip movement does not need to be exaggerated; it will naturally increase with an increase in strength, flexibility, and coordination that will come with regular walking at progressively faster speeds. (See Assessment 8-6.)

## TECHNIQUE 7: LEG GLIDE

Incorporating the leg glide technique into your walking movement will add even more to your relaxation and stride length. At the point of contact your leg should be straight, but not rigidly locked into extension. Reach out with the front leg and make contact with the ground using the longest practical stride. Then glide smoothly across your leg and foot finishing with your leg extended and a final push-off from your toes before bending at the knee and swinging your leg forward.

Technique 7: Leg glide.

When you master this technique, you will feel as if you are gliding smoothly across the ground. You will not feel an up-and-down motion or a start-and-stop motion, only a smooth, fluid gliding motion when you walk. (See Assessment 8-7.)

## TECHNIQUE 8: THE RACEWALK

Racewalking is an advanced skill that requires accelerated arm and leg speed. It is a combination of all of the previous techniques.

# Fitness Tip

## Improving Your Techniques

After you have learned these walking techniques and have become a skilled fitness walker, refer to this chapter to review the techniques. Even the most experienced competitive race walkers continue to review and improve their techniques.

Walk tall, relax, and feel your body's action. You want to stay loose to achieve optimum stride length. To racewalk, you must swing your arms and legs quickly. This is an extremely tiring technique. You will need to build up your time and distance gradually.

Two rules must be followed to prevent disqualification in competition. Racewalkers must keep one foot in contact with the ground at all times, and the support leg must be straight (not bent at the knee) in the vertical position.

Racewalking is not for beginners; it is for intermediate and advanced fitness walkers who want a higher-intensity workout. Racewalking could result in very sore muscles or injury for unconditioned beginners. (See Assessment 8-8.)

## STRATEGIES FOR HIGHER-INTENSITY WORKOUTS

Once you have mastered the basic fitness walking techniques and have developed your cardiovascular fitness to a higher level, you may find it difficult to reach your training heart rate. The following section will highlight some other strategies, besides racewalking, to help you increase your workout intensity.

There is an increased probability of soreness and injury with a sudden change in either the type or intensity of exercise. Gradually work your way into a more vigorous exercise program. High-intensity workouts should not be used by beginners.

Refer to a qualified fitness instructor if you are unsure about how to use a treadmill or stairwalking machine.

### ▶ Hill Walking

Hill walking will increase your exercise intensity and add variety to your walking routine. It will also improve your cardiovascular fitness level. Depending on the steepness of the hill, your heart rate will be higher when walking uphill. This increase in exercise heart rate makes hill walking an excellent cardiovascular conditioner and a great calorie burner.

## Fitness Walking Techniques

1. Posture and alignment
2. Heel contact
3. Heel-to-toe roll
4. Push-off
5. Arm swing
6. Hip movement
7. Leg glide
8. The racewalk

Hill walking.

## ▶ Treadmill Walking

During extreme weather conditions and at all hours of the day and night, treadmills are excellent. Treadmills offer the walker a safe walking surface and the ability to control speed and elevation. Many walkers use treadmills to complement their normal walking programs, whereas others depend on them exclusively.

## ▶ Stair Walking

Stair walking is hill walking for those who do not have hills. It is a superb exercise for the cardiovascular system. In addition to the aerobic benefits, stair walking develops muscular strength in your legs and hips, your body weight must be lifted with each step. To increase your exercise intensity and add variety to your fitness walking program, try stair walking.

Treadmill walking.

Stair walking.

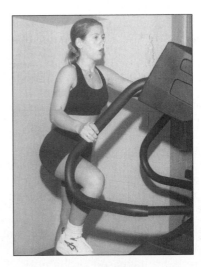

Stair walking.

Water walking.

## ▶ Water Walking

Especially during the hot weather months, walking in water offers the triple bonus of exercise, less shock impact, and a refreshing environment. When music is added, the water walker feels even more ready to swing those legs and pump those arms. Striding through the water provides a cardiovascular workout and can use more calories than land walking. At three miles an hour in thigh-deep water, you will use approximately 460 calories versus 240 for land walking. Next time you're at a pool, give water walking a try.

## SUMMARY

- To receive optimum benefits from fitness walking, it is necessary to walk at a brisk pace.
- Adopting specific techniques for fitness walking will increase your speed, stride length, and efficiency.
- Strategies for higher-intensity workouts include hill walking, treadmill walking, stair walking, and water walking.
- High-intensity workouts, including racewalking, are not recommended for beginners.
- There is an increased probability of soreness with a sudden change in either the type or intensity of exercise.
- For those unsure how to use a treadmill or stair walking machine, refer to a qualified fitness instructor.

# Assessment 8-1

## Posture and Alignment

Name _____  Section _____  Date _____

The purpose of this assessment is to learn correct body alignment for fitness walking.

Assume a standing position, with correct body alignment for fitness walking. Have a partner evaluate each guideline and place a check in either the "Yes" or "No" column.

| Guidelines | Yes | No |
|---|---|---|
| Head and neck erect | _____ | _____ |
| Eyes straight ahead | _____ | _____ |
| Shoulders pulled back and relaxed | _____ | _____ |
| Back straight | _____ | _____ |
| Chest lifted up | _____ | _____ |
| Abdomen pulled in | _____ | _____ |
| Buttocks tucked in | _____ | _____ |
| Elbows down at side | _____ | _____ |
| Elbows bent at 90-degree angle | _____ | _____ |
| Palms facing inward | _____ | _____ |
| Hands in relaxed fist position | _____ | _____ |

Did you demonstrate correct body alignment for fitness walking? _____

If not, which areas do you need to focus on? _____

# Assessment 8-2

Name                                    Section              Date

The purpose of this assessment is to emphasize the idea of landing on your heel first, as opposed to landing flatfooted or on the ball of your foot.

Read "Technique 2: Heel Contact" in chapter 8. Walk 10 steps. Have a partner check to see if you are contacting the ground with your heel first.

Did you contact the ground with your heel first? _____

If not, what part of your foot made contact with the ground first? _____

Practice walking at a slower pace until you are able to make contact with your heel first.

# Assessment 8-3

_____     _____     _____
Name                                          Section           Date

The purpose of this assessment is to experience the heel-to-toe roll.

Read "Technique 3: Heel-to-Toe Roll" in chapter 8. Walk 10 steps. Have a partner watch your heel-to-toe roll. After your heel makes contact with the ground, roll your foot forward. Keep the weight toward the outer edge of your foot. Continue to roll forward until you push off with your toes.

Were you able to roll across your foot from heel-to-toe? _____

# Assessment 8-4

Name           Section       Date

The purpose of this assessment is to emphasize the push-off.

Read "Technique 4: Push-Off" in chapter 8. Raise yourself on the toes of both feet at the same time. Repeat this five times. Next, practice the push-off by walking a short distance with an exaggerated push-off. Push all the way up on your toes before breaking contact with the ground. Have a partner watch to see if you are pushing off with your toes or picking up your foot early.

Did you push off from your toes? _____

# Assessment 8-5

## Practicing the Arm Swing

Name            Section      Date

The purpose of this assessment is to focus your attention on your arm swing while fitness walking.

Read "Technique 5: Arm Swing" in chapter 8. Using proper posture and alignment, practice the arm swing while walking. Start slowly, and gradually increase the speed of your arms as you increase your walking speed.

Have a partner check to make sure your arm swing is correct.

Were you able to walk at progressively faster speeds and keep your arm swing coordinated with your leg speed? _____

# Assessment 8-6

## Increasing Stride Length

Name                                    Section          Date

   The purpose of this assessment is to increase your stride length.

   Read "Technique 6: Hip Movement" in chapter 8. From the ready position, take one giant step forward, extending your right leg as far forward as it will comfortably go. Hold this position for 3 seconds; then lift your right foot and move it another three to five inches forward. Hold this new position for 10 seconds. Return to the ready position and repeat the procedure with your left leg. Perform this activity five times with each leg. Practicing this will help increase your stride length.

   Have a partner measure your normal walking stride from the heel of your forward foot to the toes of your back foot. Then measure your stride after allowing your hips to follow through. Remember to keep your foot in contact with the ground as long as possible. Now compare the measurements to discover the extra distance in your stride length when you include the hip movement. Place the measurements in the following blanks.

_____ Normal walking stride measurement.

_____ Measurement after allowing your hips to follow through.

_____ Difference in measurements.

# Assessment 8-7

Name                    Section         Date

The purpose of this assessment is to emphasize the feeling of a smooth walking technique.

Have a partner watch you walk at progressively faster speeds. If possible, have someone make a videotape of you walking at progressively faster speeds.

Did you have an up-and-down motion? _____

Did you have a start-and-stop motion? _____

Was there anything jerky about your technique? _____

Were you able to glide smoothly as you increased your walking speed? _____

# Assessment 8-8

Name                                    Section                    Date

The purpose of this assessment is to learn how to add speed to your fitness walking. This technique is especially important if you plan to increase the intensity of your workouts.

Read "Technique 8: The Racewalk" in chapter 8. After you have warmed up properly, and have walked for several minutes, move your arms and legs faster while you walk. Begin by racewalking for short distances. For recovery, use a slower pace between these sprints. Gradually increase the distance you can racewalk as you increase your cardiovascular endurance and leg strength.

Next, count the number of racewalk steps you can take in one minute. An easy way to find your steps per minute is to count how many steps you take with your right foot in one minute and multiply by two. This is much easier than trying to count every step when you are walking at fast speeds. The maximum effective leg speed you will probably be able to achieve with a four-foot stride is about 200 steps per minute. For most fitness walking workouts, a range of 130 to 180 steps per minute is good.

How many steps per minute do you take during your normal fitness walking workout? _____

How many steps per minute can you take when you walk as fast as possible for one minute? _____

(Caution: This is a risky assessment for unfit beginners. Make sure you are healthy and fit before you try racewalking at your maximum speed.)

# CHAPTER 9

## STRATEGIES FOR HEALTHY NUTRITION

## OBJECTIVES

*After reading this chapter, you should be able to do the following:*

- Define nutrition and understand its relationship to wellness.
- Discuss the importance of balance, variety, and moderation for healthy nutrition.
- Identify and describe the six classes of nutrients.
- Describe the Food Guide Pyramid and the Dietary Guidelines for Americans.
- Explain how to read a food label.
- Investigate the concerns about fast foods.
- Interpret the 80/20 rule for healthy nutrition.

## KEY TERMS

*While reading this chapter, you will become familiar with the following terms:*

- ► Appetite
- ► Calorie
- ► Complex Carbohydrates

- ► Fiber
- ► Glucose
- ► Hunger

*Continued*

**125**

## KEY TERMS

*Continued from p. 125*

- ► **Kilocalorie**
- ► **Nutrition**
- ► **Saturated Fats**
- ► **Simple Carbohydrates**
- ► **Trans-fatty Acids**
- ► **Unsaturated Fats**

Each day we have many choices to make about food: when to eat, what to eat, and how much to eat. We have to eat and drink to stay alive. This is one lifestyle behavior that is mandatory. The key is to eat and drink for energy and health, not only for pleasure and convenience. Our eating patterns play a major role in our level of well-being.

Nutrition experts agree that healthy nutrition is built on balance, variety, and moderation. This means enjoying many different foods in moderate portions without giving up your favorite selections. A healthy diet can prevent the consumption of too many calories, too much of any one nutrient, or too much of any single food.

The college years often bring about changes in food patterns. Factors such as class attendance, long study hours, work, finances, and extracurricular activities can interfere with healthy eating patterns. As a result of busy schedules, college students become more dependent on fast foods, delivery services, and vending machines to satisfy appetite and supply energy.

## WHAT IS NUTRITION?

**Nutrition** comes from the Latin word that means *to nourish,* or providing all that is necessary to sustain life. Human nutrition, therefore, is defined as the science of food, the study of its uses within the body, and its relationship to health. Proper nutrition sustains life by promoting good health.

The study of nutrition involves knowing about approximately 46 essential nutrients, which fall into six major categories: *carbohydrates, fats, proteins, vitamins, minerals,* and *water.* Nutrition is concerned with how the body uses these nutrients and their effects on your health. Positive nutritional behavior includes choosing the daily recommended servings from the Food Guide Pyramid and following the dietary guidelines recommended for Americans by the U.S. Department of Agriculture.

# NUTRITION AND WELLNESS

Proper nutrition has long been considered an important factor contributing to a healthy lifestyle. Positive nutritional practices can enhance growth, development, and optimal health. In addition, eating well can improve vitality, enhance quality of life, and lead to greater life expectancy. On the other hand, unhealthy nutritional behaviors such as high-fat diets can be a contributing factor to such problems as heart disease, cancer, stroke, diabetes, obesity, gallstones, and arthritis.

Although the act of eating is a voluntary activity, it becomes habitual because it is given little thought. More than a thousand times a year, you choose to eat a meal. In your lifetime, you will consume more than seventy thousand meals. Imagine how many thousands of pounds of food! In one day, your eating selections may affect your health only slightly, but in the long term they become cumulative.

Most people need to distinguish between **hunger** and **appetite.** Hunger is the physiological need for food, while appetite is the desire to eat. The physiological need by your body for food is often satisfied much sooner than is your appetite.

► **Appetite**
The desire to eat.

► **Calorie**
The energy-producing value of food when oxidized in the body.

► **Complex Carbohydrates**
Foods made up of starches, such as pasta and rice, that the body uses for long-term energy.

► **Fiber**
Made up of indigestable carbohydrates that offer health benefits.

► **Glucose**
A sugar used by the body's cells for energy.

► **Hunger**
The physiological need for food.

► **Kilocalorie**
The amount of heat (or energy) required to raise the temperature of 1 *kilogram* (or 1,000 grams) of water by 1° Celsius.

► **Nutrition**
The science of food, the study of its uses within the body, and its relationship to health.

► **Saturated Fats**
Substances that usually come from animal sources, solid at room temperature, and associated with health problems.

► **Simple Carbohydrates**
Foods easily absorbed by the body's cells; provide only short-term energy.

► **Trans-Fatty Acid**
Fats that result when liquid oil has hydrogen added to it to make it more solid (hydrogeneation).

► **Unsaturated Fats**
Substances found in plant sources, liquid at room temperature, and associated with health benefits.

Over time the consequences of your eating selections become cumulative.

To promote good health, we need to eat what we believe to be an adequate portion, then wait 15 minutes to see if we are still hungry.

Food affects all dimensions of wellness. Most people view food as only affecting the physical dimension of wellness, when actually it influences all dimensions (see figure 9-1). To a large degree, our social dimension is centered around food—not around nutrition. The good host offers guests something to eat and drink. What, for instance, would a party or casual get-together be like without food or drink? Food can be used also to comfort us emotionally when we are sad or upset, or it can be used as a reward during happy times. These are a few examples of the use of food in society.

## CALORIES (KILOCALORIES)

The term **calorie** is used to indicate the energy-producing value of food when oxidized in the body. When discussing nutrition, we use *Calorie* (with a capital C), which is actually a **kilocalorie (kcal),** and is defined as the amount of heat (or energy) required to raise the temperature of 1 *kilogram* (or 1000 grams) of water by 1°Celsius. If an apple, therefore, contains a hundred Calories, it provides a hundred units of energy. See table 9-1 for the caloric values of nutrients and how they apply to each nutrient.

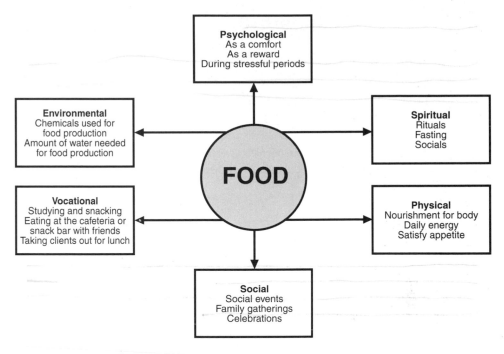

**FIGURE 9-1** Food affects all wellness components.

## TABLE 9-1
### The Caloric Value of Nutrients

| Nutrient | Calories |
|---|---|
| 1 gram of protein | 4 |
| 1 gram of carbohydrates (sugar or starch) | 4 |
| 1 gram of alcohol | 7 |
| 1 gram of fat | 9 |
| Vitamins, minerals, water, fiber | 0 |

**How to Apply the Caloric Value to Each Nutrient**

A serving of microwave popping corn (3 cups popped) contains 17 grams of carbohydrate, 3 grams of protein, 8 grams of fat, and 152 calories.

**Carbohydrate:**

17 grams × 4 calories per gram = 68 calories from carbohydrate (68 ÷ 152 = 45%)

**Protein:**

3 grams × 4 calories per gram = 12 calories from protein (12 ÷ 152 = 8%)

**Fat:**

8 grams × 9 calories per gram = 72 calories from fat (72 ÷ 152 = 47%)

1 serving of microwave popping corn = 152 calories (45% carbohydrates, 8% proteins, and 47% fat)

# THE SIX CLASSES OF NUTRIENTS

The six classes of nutrients are carbohydrates, fats, proteins, vitamins, minerals, and water (see figure 9-2). Nutrients perform three functions. First, nutrients such as carbohydrates, fats, and proteins provide energy for the body. Protein's major function, however, is to build and repair tissue rather than be used as a major source of energy. Second, protein and certain minerals, such as calcium, are nutrients that help build and maintain body tissue. Finally, nutrients such as protein, vitamins, minerals, and water help regulate body functions; for example, oxygen attaches to the iron molecules of hemoglobin and is carried to the body's cells.

## ▶ Carbohydrates

Carbohydrates contribute about half of the body's energy needs, without which no other metabolic activity could occur. They do so in the form of **glucose,** a sugar into which all carbohydrates eventually break down. Glucose is the most important sugar for the cells of the human body.

**FIGURE 9-2** The six classes of nutrients needed for wellness.

There are two major types of carbohydrates. The first is called **complex carbo-hydrates.** They are made up of starches, the form of nutrients easiest for the body to digest, absorb, and use. Because of this, starches are the staple food for most of the world. Foods such as pasta; rice; whole grain breads; cereals; and starchy vegetables, such as corn, potatoes, and winter squash provide rich sources of car-bohydrates. Besides providing long-term, or sustained, energy, these complex carbohydrates also supply the body with other desirable nutrients, including water, protein, fiber, vitamins, and minerals.

The second type of carbohydrate is labeled **simple carbohydrates** because of their molecular structure. These are the sugars, which also provide energy to the body, but for a shorter period of time than do the starches. All carbohydrates, simple and complex, are changed into glucose before being used as energy by the body. Other sugars in our diet include *fructose* (found in fruits, honey, and maple syrup), *sucrose* (table sugar), and *lactose* (milk sugar).

**Fiber,** a carbohydrate, is associated with many health benefits even though it contains no calories or energy for the body. Known also as roughage and bulk, fiber is made up of indigestible carbohydrates that pass through the digestive tract without being absorbed. We are not able to digest fiber because the body lacks an enzyme to break it down. Table 9-2 highlights the two types of fiber, along with their sources and possible health benefits.

With a well-balanced diet, you are likely to get the different types of fiber and all their benefits. To consume enough fiber to enhance your health (25–35 grams daily), eat a well-balanced diet, making sure you consume ample amounts of

**TABLE 9-2**
**Possible Health Benefits of Fiber**

| Fiber Type | Source | Possible Benefits |
|---|---|---|
| *Insoluble* | Brown rice<br>Dried beans<br>Fruits<br>Popcorn<br>Rye<br>Seeds<br>Vegetables<br>Wheat bran<br>Whole grains | Promotes regularity<br>Protects against colon cancer<br>Prevents obesity by replacing dietary fat<br>Manages blood sugar |
| *Soluble* | Barley<br>Dried beans<br>Fruits<br>Oat bran<br>Oatmeal<br>Rye<br>Seeds<br>Vegetables | Lowers blood cholesterol<br>Manages blood sugar<br>Prevents obesity by replacing dietary fat |

whole grains, fruits, and vegetables daily. Some benefits from a high-fiber diet may come from the food containing the fiber, not from the fiber alone. Thus, it is better to receive fiber from foods rather than from supplements. To prevent intestinal problems such as bloating and gas, experts recommend increasing fiber gradually in the diet while drinking plenty of water.

## ▶ Fats

A small amount of fat is required for good health. Fats (also known as *lipids*) provide energy, carry the fat-soluble vitamins A, D, E, and K in the blood; provide essential fatty acids needed for growth; insulate the body; are essential parts of every cell; and contribute to hormone synthesis and the blood-clotting mechanism. Unfortunately, people of all ages take in too much fat, leading to serious health problems. Health experts recommend that people, especially those at risk for heart disease, eat less fat. It is recommended that *no more than 30 percent* of your calories should come from fat, of which no more than *10 percent* come from saturated fat choices (i.e., meats, milk, and milk products).

There are two types of fats in foods—saturated and unsaturated. **Saturated fats,** except for the tropical oils, come from animal sources and are usually solid at room temperature. It is this type of fat that is associated with heart disease and cancer of the breast, colon, and prostate. Saturated fats are found in meats, butter, milk, and in the tropical oils: palm, palm kernel, and coconut.

The average American adult consumes 115 pounds of fat per year.

**Unsaturated fats** are found in plant sources and are liquid at room temperature. Two classes of unsaturated fats are *polyunsaturated* (corn, safflower, sesame, soybean, sunflower, and cottonseed oils) and *monounsaturated* (olive, peanut, and canola oils). Research shows that polyunsaturated fats may also be unhealthy because they lower the "good" *high density lipoproteins (HDL)* cholesterol and may increase risk for certain types of cancer. This leaves monosaturated oils as the fat of choice. They have been shown to lower the "bad" *low density lipoproteins (LDL)* cholesterol but maintain the HDL cholesterol levels.

Recent studies are showing that foods such as margarine and shortening containing hydrogenated fats or **trans-fatty acids** can result in higher total cholesterol and LDL levels. This finding suggests that you should limit trans fats in your diet by reading labels and avoiding processed foods.

Cholesterol is a waxy, fatlike substance essential for life. Cholesterol is used to form cell membranes, the sex hormones estrogen and progesterone, and other vital substances. Cholesterol also ensures proper functioning of the nervous system. It is not a required nutrient because the body manufactures all the cholesterol it needs. Excess dietary cholesterol is linked to heart disease and strokes. Cholesterol is found in all animal foods, including meat, eggs, fish, poultry, and dairy products.

Cholesterol is carried in the bloodstream by LDLs and HDLs. The LDLs are believed to deposit cholesterol on artery walls, potentially causing coronary heart disease. HDLs are thought to carry cholesterol away from the cells in the arteries and transport it back to the liver for processing or removal.

Other studies have shown that the most significant factor in food that affects blood cholesterol is saturated fat in the diet, rather than dietary cholesterol. It has been shown that when saturated fat is introduced into the body (via diet), the liver produces cholesterol, thus raising both fat and cholesterol in the blood. These studies suggest reducing total fat in the diet and exercising to lower risk of heart disease (see table 9-3).

**TABLE 9-3**
**Strategies for Reducing Dietary Fat**

1. Consume more grains, vegetables, and fruits.
2. Stick to recommended servings for meats (2–3 servings daily).
3. Substitute low-fat milk for whole milk.
4. Remove chicken skin before cooking or eating.
5. Substitute low-fat yogurt or sherbet for ice cream.
6. Purchase only lean meat cuts and trim visible fats.
7. Grill, bake, or broil instead of frying.
8. Use egg whites and limit egg yolks.
9. Limit salad dressing.
10. Limit high-fat snacks and desserts.
11. Have meatless meals once or twice a week.

About half of all adults have cholesterol levels that are too high. An estimated 25 percent of Americans have high cholesterol and another 25 percent are borderline-high. Have you had your blood cholesterol levels checked recently? If not, make an appointment with your physician. Ask to receive a complete "lipid profile," which includes total cholesterol, LDL, HDL, a ratio of total cholesterol to HDL, and triglycerides.

## ▶ Protein

Protein is needed for growth, repair, and maintenance of all body cells. Protein also transmits hereditary characteristics and helps form the hormones and enzymes used to regulate body processes. Protein can be found in animal sources (meat, eggs, fish, and dairy products) and plant sources (dried beans and peas, whole grains, pasta, rice, and seeds).

Protein is made up of 20 different amino acids. It is essential that nine of the amino acids be included in your diet, because your body cannot produce them. These nine essential amino acids must be present during the same meal for growth and repair of tissue to occur. The other eleven amino acids will be produced by the body. All 20 amino acids must be present in your body at the same time to form protein.

The two types of protein are called complete and incomplete. Complete protein comes from animal sources and contains all nine of the essential amino acids. One way to get all the amino acids you need is to include foods from animal sources in your daily diet. Incomplete protein comes from plant foods (vegetables and grains) and lacks one or more of the essential amino acids. If you do not eat meat products, you can still form complete protein by combining plant proteins with each other or with animal protein. Common examples of combining proteins include cereal and milk, rice and beans, macaroni and cheese, and peanut butter and jelly on whole wheat bread.

Most Americans take in more protein than necessary for good health. Your daily protein requirements are 0.8 grams per kilogram (2.2 pounds) of body weight. This amounts to no more than 12 to 15 percent of your total daily calories. A simple way to get a rough estimate of your protein needs is to take your weight and divide by three. If you weigh 150 pounds, your approximate daily protein needs would be 50 grams.

## ▶ Vitamins

Vitamins are organic substances needed by the body in trace amounts. Vitamins work by enhancing the action of enzymes in the body. This enables us to use other nutrients. There are thirteen known vitamins, each responsible for performing a variety of specific and unique roles within the body. Vitamins help regulate important bodily functions such as manufacturing healthy blood cells and liberating energy from carbohydrates, fats, and proteins.

The two types of vitamins are water-soluble and fat-soluble. The vitamin B-complex and vitamin C can be dissolved in water (water-soluble) and are more readily eliminated from the body. Vitamins A, D, E, and K are transported, absorbed, and stored with body fat (fat-soluble). Fat-soluble vitamins are not quickly eliminated, therefore excessive amounts can lead to toxic, health-threatening effects. Research has shown that megadosing with certain water-soluble vitamins has also resulted in side effects.

Certain people can benefit from taking vitamin supplements. Vegetarians, pregnant or breast-feeding women, women with excessive menstrual bleeding, strict dieters, and those not following a well-balanced diet should check with their physician about vitamin and mineral supplementation. In addition, those suffering from long-term illness and disease or taking medication that reduces appetite or hinders the body's ability to use nutrients should consult with their physicians.

Folic acid, a B-vitamin, has become increasingly important in our diet to help prevent birth defects along with heart disease and stroke. Research has documented the importance for all women of childbearing age and those individuals with risk factors for health disease and stroke to consume 400 micrograms of folic acid (the Recommended Dietary Allowance) every day either through diet or supplementation. Because of its increasing importance, the FDA is considering adding folic acid to flour. This, in turn, would fortify such products as breads, pasta, and cereals. In the meantime, consume foods from table 9-4 or consider supplementation.

## TABLE 9-4
## Good Sources of Folic Acid

| Food | Folic Acid (micrograms) |
|---|---|
| *Total* cereal (3/4 cup) | 400 |
| Lentils (1/2 cup, cooked) | 179 |
| Pinto Beans (1/2 cup, cooked) | 145 |
| Chickpeas (1/2 cup, cooked) | 145 |
| Spinach (1/2 cup, cooked) | 131 |
| Kidney Beans (1/2 cup, cooked) | 115 |
| Orange juice (1 cup, from concentrate) | 109 |
| Spinach (1 cup, raw) | 109 |
| Most breakfast cereals (1 cup) | 100 |
| Romaine lettuce (1 cup, shredded) | 76 |
| Split peas (1/2 cup, cooked) | 64 |
| Broccoli (1/2 cup, cooked) | 39 |

Data from: USDA Handbook 8.

## ▶ The Antioxidant Supplement Debate

The antioxidants of vitamin C, vitamin E, and beta carotene have developed a reputation for their ability to protect us against our natural oxidative processes and ravages of the environment. Due to breathing and the normal oxidation of our cells, the body constantly produces reactive chemicals called *free radicals*. During vigorous exercise, the rate of production for free radicals increases, and the body also acquires them from environmental sources such as cigarette smoke and air pollution. The problem with free radicals is that they are unstable and wreak havoc on our normal cells. The damage caused by free radicals is believed to contribute to such conditions as heart disease, cancer, and aging. Antioxidants may protect the body from this damage by neutralizing the free radicals. Numerous studies have indicated that people who consume a diet high in antioxidant fruits and vegetables are less likely to develop diseases related to free radicals.

The jury is still out on supplements. Conflicting study results have led some to abandon antioxidants because they can often act as pro-oxidants in supplements, boosting oxidant and free-radical production. Others, notably Dr. Kenneth Cooper, the highly respected father of the aerobics movement, claim we need them more than ever, especially if we enjoy vigorous exercise. While further research is needed, it is safe to suggest that you should eat plenty of antioxidant-rich foods (see table 9-5). If you still feel you are not getting enough antioxidants from food, take a supplement, but do so in moderation.

## ▶ Minerals

Minerals perform many vital functions in the body. From building strong bones and teeth (calcium) to forming hemoglobin in red blood cells (iron), minerals are essential for good nutrition. Like vitamins, minerals are needed in small

**TABLE 9-5**
**Selected Foods That Contain Antioxidants**

| Vitamin C | Vitamin E | Carotenoids (Beta-Carotene) | Mixed Antioxidants |
|---|---|---|---|
| Cabbage | Almonds | Apricots | Bran wheat |
| Cauliflower | Chick peas | Broccoli | Cloves |
| Grapefruit | Eggs | Cantaloupe | Green tea |
| Oranges | Hazelnuts | Carrots | Nutmeg |
| Peppers | Oatmeal | Kale | Pepper |
| Potatoes | Rye flour | Mustard greens | Rice |
| Raspberries | Soybeans | Spinach | Sesame |
| Strawberries | Sunflower seeds | Sweet potatoes | Thyme |
| Tangerines | Wheat germ | Winter squash | |

amounts and do not supply energy. Other important functions include assisting in nerve transmission and muscle contraction and regulating fluid levels and the acid-base balance of the body. Minerals can also be toxic in excess amounts. In the adult diet, mineral concerns include too much sodium and, for women, too little iron and calcium.

Minerals are classified into two types: major and trace. Calcium, sodium, phosphorous, chloride, potassium, and magnesium are considered major minerals because they are needed in amounts greater than 100 milligrams per day. Trace minerals such as iron, zinc, iodine, selenium, and copper are needed only in small amounts. Minerals are absorbed, used, and eliminated by the body, so it is important to replace them daily. Eating a wide variety of nutritious foods is the best way to obtain sufficient quantities of the essential minerals. Fruits and vegetables are ideal mineral sources.

## ▶ Water

Water is often called the "forgotten nutrient." Water may be our most important nutrient because without it we would not live more than a week. More than half our body weight comes from water. Water provides the medium for nutrient and waste transportation and plays a vital role in nearly all biochemical reactions in the body. People seldom think about the importance of an adequate daily intake of water.

Adults require eight glasses of water a day and even more with an active lifestyle. If you eat more fresh fruits and vegetables, you will require less water. Three sound recommendations for drinking more water include keeping a container of water in the refrigerator, drinking water throughout the day, and drinking water instead of beverages when dining out. Good choices are plain water from the tap and any kind of mineral water or bottled water. Many people put lemon or lime in their water to give it added flavor. Sweetened drinks (fruit drinks, soda), coffee, tea, and alcohol should be limited. Caffeine and alcohol increase dehydration and necessitate an increase in water intake.

For good health drink plenty of water.

## FOOD GUIDE PYRAMID

The U.S. Departments of Agriculture and Health and Human Services have adopted the Food Guide Pyramid. The Food Guide Pyramid can help you choose the recommended servings from healthy foods to get the nutrients you need without excess calories, fats, cholesterol, sugar, or sodium.

The Food Guide Pyramid provides a simple, practical guide for general meal planning and can be used to evaluate your overall food intake pattern. The pyramid illustrates the five food groups with recommended servings importa to a healthy diet (see figure 9-3). The diagram places the bread, cereal, rice, and pasta group at the base, taking up the largest section. Rich in complex carbohydrates, this group serves as the foundation of the diet. Vegetables and fruits are two equal groups instead of one and have the next largest sections. Above them as the pyramid narrows, meats and dairy products share a band. At the top are fats, oils, and sweets, considered a food category rather than a food group. This category is the smallest and should provide the fewest calories.

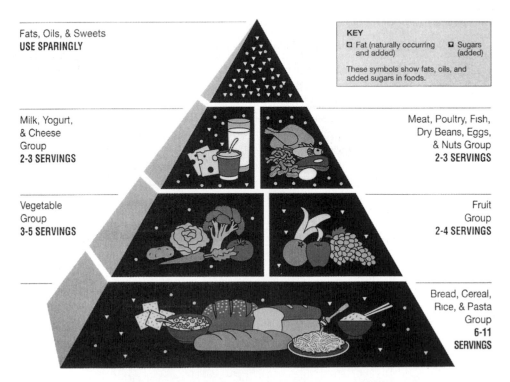

**FIGURE 9-3** The USDA Food Guide Pyramid.

## THE NEW 2000 DIETARY GUIDELINES FOR AMERICANS

To further guide your healthy nutritional patterns, the U.S. Department of Health and Human Services have issued new Dietary Guidelines for Americans. Follow these guidelines to promote your health and reduce your disease risk. The 10 dietary guidelines are classified into the "ABC's for Health."

**A** im for Fitness.
**B** uild a Healthy Base.
**C** hoose Sensibly.

*Aim for Fitness*—The two guidelines in this category emphasize a lifestyle that combines wise food choices with regular physical activity.

1. Aim for a healthy weight (see chapter 10).
2. Be physically active every day (at least 30 minutes most days and preferably every day).

# Fitness Tip

### Keeping Your Food Safe to Eat

Follow these steps to meet guideline 6:

1. Wash hands and surfaces often.
2. Separate raw, cooked, and ready-to-eat foods while shopping, preparing, and storing.
3. Cook food to a safe temperature. Use a thermometer when cooking animal products.
4. Refrigerate perishable foods promptly:
   a. within two hours of purchasing or preparing
   b. within one hour if the air temperature is above 90° F.
   c. use refrigerated leftovers within three–four days.
5. Follow safety instructions in the label.
6. Serve meat, poultry, eggs, and fish just before eating, and chill leftovers as soon as you are finished. Keep hot foods above 140° F and cold foods below 40° F.
7. If in doubt, throw it out. If food has been left out for too long or refrigerated for too long, it may not be safe to eat even if it looks and smells fine.

*Build a Healthy Base*—The four guidelines in this category provide a foundation for healthy eating.

3. Let the Food Guide Pyramid guide your food choices.
4. Eat a variety of grains daily, especially whole grains.
5. Eat a variety of fruits and vegetables daily.
6. Keep food safe to eat.

*Choose Sensibly*—The four guidelines in this category can help you make sensible decisions that promote your health and reduce your risk of certain chronic diseases.

7. Choose a diet low in saturated fat and cholesterol and moderate (no more than 30 percent of calories) in total fat.
8. Choose beverages and foods to moderate your intake of sugars. While sugar does not cause hyperactivity, it can promote tooth decay and weight gain.
9. Choose and prepare foods with less salt (can help reduce your chance of developing high blood pressure).
10. If you drink alcoholic beverages, do so in moderation.

## THE 80/20 RULE

Another guide to follow for healthy nutrition is the 80/20 rule. The 80/20 rule states that if you eat a variety of nutritious foods 80 percent of the time, you can eat whatever you want for the remaining 20 percent and not feel guilty. If your diet is consistently nutritious, an occasional hot dog or milk shake isn't going to adversely affect you. Unfortunately, too many people follow the 20/80 rule that is, they eat healthy 20 percent of the time and unhealthy 80 percent of the time.

# Fitness Tip

### Moderating Your Intake of Sugars

Follow these steps to meet guideline 8:

1. Keep your teeth and gums healthy by rinsing your mouth after you eat sugar or starches, including dried fruit.
2. Brush and floss your teeth regularly.
3. Limit your consumption of foods with added sugars.
4. Drink water rather than sweetened drinks.
5. Don't let sodas and other sweets crowd out more nutritious foods, such as low-fat milk or other sources of calcium.

Those who follow the 20/80 rule have diets high in calories, fat, saturated fat, cholesterol, sugar, and sodium, and low in grains, fruits, and vegetables. Knowing their diet is low in nutrients, some people compensate by adding vitamins, fiber, and an occasional bean sprout. Though it is wise to consider your nutritional needs carefully, it is not wise to lean on a magic bullet vitamin to rescue an out-of-balance diet. What kind of eater are you? Are you more likely to follow the 80/20 rule, the 20/80 rule, or another rule?

## FAST FOODS

For many people, especially college students, fast foods have become a way of life. The nutritional value of fast foods, from cheeseburgers to leanburgers, can vary greatly. Breakfast foods, potatoes, whole wheat breads, salad bars, low-fat meat and milk products, low-calorie foods, and vegetable oils are examples of how fast-food companies have expanded their offerings and made foods more nutritious. However, one glance at the menu still finds the majority of fast foods high in calories, fat, saturated fat, cholesterol, sodium, and sugar. Frying foods such as french fries and chicken breasts in oil is one reason for the high level of fat in fast foods.

Many fast-food chains provide nutritional information for their customers. This information can keep you abreast of your nutrient intake, thereby preventing you from exceeding any maximum levels. Although fast foods can be nutritious, it would be unhealthy and expensive to rely on these foods as your main source of nutrition. *Once again, moderation is the key.*

## FOOD LABELS

Reading food labels is the best way to judge the contributions of individual foods to your daily diet and health goals. Many shoppers compare prices, but few compare labels before selecting foods (see figure 9-4).

## SUMMARY

- Experts agree that healthy nutrition is based upon balance, variety, and moderation.
- The six major categories of nutrients are carbohydrates, proteins, fats, vitamins, minerals, and water.
- Proper nutrition is considered an important behavior for a healthy lifestyle. The key is to eat and drink for health and energy levels, and not only for pleasure.
- The Food Guide Pyramid can guide your number of servings from each of the five food groups.

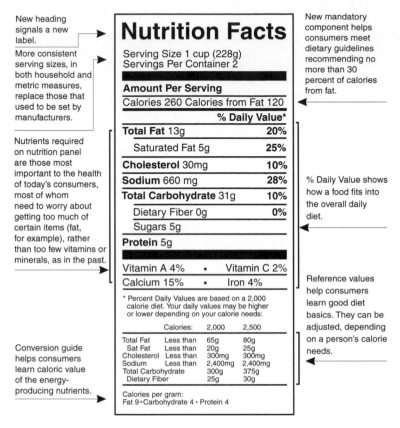

New heading signals a new label.

More consistent serving sizes, in both household and metric measures, replace those that used to be set by manufacturers.

Nutrients required on nutrition panel are those most important to the health of today's consumers, most of whom need to worry about getting too much of certain items (fat, for example), rather than too few vitamins or minerals, as in the past.

Conversion guide helps consumers learn caloric value of the energy-producing nutrients.

New mandatory component helps consumers meet dietary guidelines recommending no more than 30 percent of calories from fat.

% Daily Value shows how a food fits into the overall daily diet.

Reference values help consumers learn good diet basics. They can be adjusted, depending on a person's calorie needs.

# Nutrition Facts

Serving Size 1 cup (228g)
Servings Per Container 2

**Amount Per Serving**

Calories 260 Calories from Fat 120

**% Daily Value***

| | |
|---|---|
| **Total Fat** 13g | **20%** |
| Saturated Fat 5g | **25%** |
| **Cholesterol** 30mg | **10%** |
| **Sodium** 660 mg | **28%** |
| **Total Carbohydrate** 31g | **10%** |
| Dietary Fiber 0g | **0%** |
| Sugars 5g | |
| **Protein** 5g | |

| | | |
|---|---|---|
| Vitamin A 4% | • | Vitamin C 2% |
| Calcium 15% | • | Iron 4% |

* Percent Daily Values are based on a 2,000 calorie diet. Your daily values may be higher or lower depending on your calorie needs:

| | Calories: | 2,000 | 2,500 |
|---|---|---|---|
| Total Fat | Less than | 65g | 80g |
| Sat Fat | Less than | 20g | 25g |
| Cholesterol | Less than | 300mg | 300mg |
| Sodium | Less than | 2,400mg | 2,400mg |
| Total Carbohydrate | | 300g | 375g |
| Dietary Fiber | | 25g | 30g |

Calories per gram:
Fat 9 • Carbohydrate 4 • Protein 4

**FIGURE 9-4** Nutrition facts—macaroni and cheese.

- The newly revised dietary guidelines for Americans follow the "ABC'S for Health."
- The 80/20 rule is a general guide that can govern your food choices.
- Moderation is the key for fast foods.
- Reading labels is the best way to judge the contributions of individual foods to your daily diet and health goals.
- For more information on nutrition, visit this address: www.nal.usda.gov/fnic/dga/index.html

# Assessment 9-1

_____    _____    _____
Name                              Section         Date

   Answer the questions for each dietary part of the Nutrition Questionnaire by placing the appropriate points in the score column. Add your scores for each part and write them in the results section. Answer the four short-answer questions in the results section.

## PART I. EAT A VARIETY OF FOODS

   Do you eat a variety of healthy foods each day? For each question, give yourself 2 points if your answer is "always," 1 point if your answer is "usually," and 0 points if your answer is "seldom" or "never." Maximum possible points = 10.

## SCORE

1. _____ I eat at least six servings every day from the breads, cereals, rice, and pasta group.
2. _____ I eat at least three servings every day from the vegetable group.
3. _____ I eat at least two servings every day from the fruit group.
4. _____ I have a minimum of two but not more than three servings each day from the milk, yogurt, and cheese group (keep the point(s) if your servings above three are low-fat).
5. _____ I have a minimum of two but not more than three servings each day from the meat, poultry, fish, dry beans, and nuts group.

_____ Total

## PART II. MAINTAIN HEALTHY WEIGHT

Are you maintaining healthy weight? If you are, give yourself 10 points. If not, give yourself 0 points. Maximum possible points = 10.

\_\_\_\_\_ Are you within your recommended weight range? See table 10-1 in chapter 10.

\_\_\_\_\_ Total

## PART III. CHOOSE A DIET LOW IN FAT, SATURATED FAT, AND CHOLESTEROL

Is your diet low in fat, saturated fat, and cholesterol? Give yourself 1 point for every "yes" answer and 0 points for every "no" answer. Maximum possible points = 10.

1. \_\_\_\_\_ My milk, yogurt, and cheese selections are mostly nonfat or low in fat (low-fat milk rather than whole milk, mozzarella cheese rather than cheddar cheese).
2. \_\_\_\_\_ I use margarine, butter, cream, or sour cream sparingly or not at all.
3. \_\_\_\_\_ I keep my servings from the meat, poultry, fish, dry beans, eggs, and nuts group to two moderate servings each day and occasionally have meatless meals.
4. \_\_\_\_\_ Before cooking and especially before eating, I remove the skin from chicken and visible fat from meat.
5. \_\_\_\_\_ I eat more fish and chicken than beef, ham, lamb, or pork.
6. \_\_\_\_\_ In preparing or ordering beef, fish, or chicken, I prefer grilling, broiling, and baking over frying.
7. \_\_\_\_\_ I choose low-fat yogurt, sherbet, or ice milk over ice cream.
8. \_\_\_\_\_ I use as little salad dressing as possible for my salads.
9. \_\_\_\_\_ When eating fast foods, I choose low-fat products (salad and fruit bar, baked potato, water) over high-fat products (cheeseburgers, french fries, shakes).
10. \_\_\_\_\_ I limit my intake of high-fat snacks and desserts (cookies, cakes, ice cream).

\_\_\_\_\_ Total

# PART IV. CHOOSE A DIET WITH PLENTY OF VEGETABLES, FRUITS, AND GRAIN PRODUCTS

Is your diet loaded with vegetables, fruits, and grains? For every "yes" answer, give yourself 1 point. For every "no" answer, give yourself 0 points. Maximum possible points = 10.

1. _____ I like the taste of vegetables and enjoy eating them daily.
2. _____ I like the taste of fruits and enjoy eating them daily.
3. _____ I would prefer a vegetable or fruit snack over any other snack.
4. _____ If the option were available, I would choose fruit dessert over any other dessert.
5. _____ If I realize during the evening I have not consumed the recommended daily number of vegetable (three) and fruit (two) servings, I will strive to correct the deficiency that night or the next day.
6. _____ If the option were available, I would choose a wheat or bran cereal over a presweetened cereal.
7. _____ If the option were available, I would choose whole wheat bread over white bread.
8. _____ I eat products made from a variety of grains, such as wheat, rice, and oats.
9. _____ I limit high-fat grains in my diet (croissants, cakes, cookies).
10. _____ I strive to eat a minimum of six servings each day of bread, cereal, rice, and pasta products.

_____ Total

# PART V. USE SUGARS ONLY IN MODERATION

What size (small, medium, large, or humongous) is your sweet tooth? For every "yes" answer to the following statements, give yourself 1 point. For every "no" answer, give yourself 0 points. Maximum possible points = 5.

1. _____ I limit sugar intake whenever possible.
2. _____ I do not like candy or chocolate.
3. _____ I would prefer cereal, tea, and coffee with no sugar or sweeteners added. (Keep the point if you don't eat cereal or drink tea or coffee.)
4. _____ I drink more water and milk than sweetened liquids such as soft drinks.
5. _____ I prefer snacks that contain no sugar, low sugar, or natural sugar (vegetables, fruits) over high-sugar snacks and desserts (cookies, cakes).

_____ Total

## PART VI. USE SALT AND SODIUM ONLY IN MODERATION

What size mountain (small, medium, or high) of salt are you on? If your answer to each of the following statements is "always" give yourself 2 points. If your answer is "usually" give yourself 1 point, and 0 points if your answer is "seldom" or "never." Maximum possible points = 4.

1. _____ I choose foods lightly salted or not salted at all.
2. _____ I add little or no salt either while cooking foods or when eating them.

_____ Total

## PART VII. IF YOU DRINK ALCOHOLIC BEVERAGES, DO SO IN MODERATION

If you drink alcohol, do you drink in moderation? For every "yes" answer, give yourself 5 points. For every "no" answer, give yourself 0 points. Maximum possible points = 10.

1. _____ I do not drink more than two alcoholic beverages in a day. One drink is 5 oz. of wine, 10 oz. wine cooler, 12 oz. beer, or 1 oz. hard liquor (whiskey, gin, rum, vodka).
2. _____ Rarely or never do I skip entire meals or major portions of meals because my stomach is full from drinking alcoholic beverages.

_____ Total

## RESULTS

After totaling your scores for each part, write them on the following blanks.

Part I.       _____
Part II.      _____
Part III.     _____
Part IV.      _____
Part V.       _____
Part VI.      _____
Part VII.     _____

Total        _____ (out of 59)

| | |
|---|---|
| 59 | Superior food selection |
| 50–59 | Healthy food selection |
| 40–49 | Not bad, but room for improvement |
| 30–39 | Below average. Consider eating for your health and not only your taste buds. |
| Below 30 | Make an appointment with your instructor, your physician, or a dietitian for immediate dietary counsel. |

Do you feel your rating accurately reflects your nutritional health? Explain.

In what dietary guidelines are you strong?

In what dietary guidelines, if any, are you weak?

What did you learn from this questionnaire? Will you apply this information to your daily food selections?

# CHAPTER 10

# HEALTHY **WEIGHT**
## AND BODY FATNESS

## OBJECTIVES

*After reading this chapter, you should be able to do the following:*

- Identify goals for the report, *Healthy People 2010.*
- Discuss reasons why Americans are not at healthy body weight and fat levels.
- Identify and describe the strategies to develop and maintain healthy body weight and fat.
- Investigate reasons to avoid weight-loss aids.

## KEY TERMS

*While reading this chapter, you will become familiar with the following terms:*

- ► FITT
- ► Motivation
- ► Obesity
- ► Percent Body Fat
- ► Relapse
- ► Underfatness

**TABLE 10-1**

**Recommended Body Weight Chart**

| Height | 19–34 Years | 35 Years and Over | Height | 19–34 Years | 35 Years and Over |
|--------|-------------|-------------------|--------|-------------|-------------------|
| 5'0" | 97–128 | 108–138 | 5'10" | 132–174 | 146–188 |
| 5'1" | 101–132 | 111–143 | 5'11" | 136–179 | 151–194 |
| 5'2" | 104–137 | 115–148 | 6'0" | 140–184 | 155–199 |
| 5'3" | 107–141 | 119–152 | 6'1" | 144–189 | 159–205 |
| 5'4" | 111–146 | 122–157 | 6'2" | 148–195 | 164–210 |
| 5'5" | 114–150 | 126–162 | 6'3" | 152–200 | 168–216 |
| 5'6" | 118–155 | 130–167 | 6'4" | 156–205 | 173–222 |
| 5'7" | 121–160 | 134–172 | 6'5" | 160–211 | 177–228 |
| 5'8" | 125–164 | 138–178 | 6'6" | 164–216 | 182–234 |
| 5'9" | 129–169 | 142–183 | | | |

The higher weights generally apply to men, who tend to have more muscle and bone; the lower weights more often apply to women.

Data from: *Dietary Guidelines for Americans.* Washington, DC: U.S. Department of Agriculture and Department of Health and Human Services, 1995.

### Key Goals from *Healthy People 2010*

- Increase prevalence of a healthy weight.
- Reduce prevalence of overweight.
- Increase proportion of people who meet national dietary guidelines.
- Increase the adoption and maintenance of daily physical activity.
- Increase teaching about nutrition and physical activity.

A recent survey showed that 96 percent of adult males and 99 percent of adult females would change something about their appearance. Their leading concern was weight loss (see table 10-1 for recommended weight ranges). Two out of three Americans want to lose weight, which is why billions of dollars a year are spent on diet books, diet drinks, diet meals, and weight-loss programs. A sedentary lifestyle of overeating, excessive television viewing, movies, and video games contributes to our present condition of unhealthy weight and body fat.

Popular magazines, pageants, and television shows and commercials have created an obsession with weight loss. The focus in our

**TABLE 10-2**
**Percent Body Fat Chart**

| Classification | Women | Men |
|---|---|---|
| Essential | <8% | <5% |
| Excellent | 11–20% | 6–15% |
| Desirable | 21–29% | 16–24% |
| Obese | >30% | >25% |

culture is on losing weight rather than fat and appearance rather than health. Because of the fascination with weight loss experienced by many Americans, the theme of this chapter will be on fat management for good health.

# PERCENT BODY FAT

The percentage of total body weight that is stored body fat is called percent *body fat.* On the other hand, *lean body weight* is the portion of total body weight composed of lean tissue, which includes muscles, tendons, bones, and so on. It is a misconception that all body fat is unhealthy, because we each need some stored body fat known as *essential fat.* This level is the minimum amount of body fat needed for good health. Essential fat is required for such important functions as shock absorption for the internal organs; temperature regulation; and transportation of the fat-soluble vitamins A, D, E, and K within the body.

While some fat is essential, an enormous health problem in our society is the number of children, adolescents, and adults who possess too much fat (see table 10-2 for the percent body fat chart).

► **FITT**
An acronym for an exercise formula that stands for Frequency, Intensity, Time, and Type.

► **Motivation**
The drive or desire to begin or continue a behavior.

► **Obesity**
An excessive amount of body fat that can lead to ill health.

► **Percent Body Fat**
The percentage of total body weight that is stored body fat.

► **Relapse**
To revert to a previous unwanted behavior.

► **Underfatness**
Too little body fat that can lead to ill health.

## OBESITY (OVERFATNESS)

**Obesity** is a condition that indicates the body has stored an excessive amount of body fat. This condition is considered a chronic, degenerative disease that kills people and costs billions of dollars annually for fat-related illnesses. There is a lack of accurate data regarding the level at which stored body fat becomes a serious health problem. However, there seems to be general agreement that men with more than 25 percent body fat and women with more than 30 percent body fat should be considered obese.

Besides having high levels of body fat, *where* people store fat may increase their risk for disease. Where the body fat is located may be even more unhealthy than the amount of excess body fat. An apple-shaped body that stores fat in the upper body may be more at risk of heart disease, hypertension, strokes, and diabetes than a pear-shaped body that stores fat in the hips and thighs.

Creeping obesity is the term used for the gradual process of people accumulating too much body fat for their health. Obesity does not occur overnight. It is months and years in the making. As we age, the extra fat accumulates as we become less active and our basal metabolic rate (BMR) decreases. BMR is the amount of energy expended at rest to sustain the vital functions of the body. For an average person, creeping obesity often results in one-half to one pound of fat gain per year.

## UNDERFATNESS

Too little fat, or **underfatness,** can be as dangerous as too much fat. Females with 8 percent or less and males with 5 percent or less body fat are considered underfat. Although it is important to be aware of the dangers for obesity, excessive concern for thinness can also be a problem. America's obsession for being thin has led to an increase in eating disorders such as anorexia nervosa, bulimia, and bulimarexia. Each disorder is considered a serious health problem and usually involves the severe restriction of food and/or regurgitation of food.

## WHY MANAGE WEIGHT AND BODY FAT?

Achieving and maintaining desirable weight and body fat are important goals of a healthy lifestyle. A healthy body will allow you to live life to the fullest, enjoying family, school, work, and leisure time. However, an obese or too thin body can adversely affect you in all wellness components and lead to a poorer quality of life.

Many physical problems are associated with being obese. Obesity is linked with several heart disease risk factors, including high blood pressure, high cholesterol, and diabetes. Certain cancers, such as breast cancer for women and prostate and colon cancer for men, are prevalent in the obese. Strokes or kidney problems may result from high blood pressure. The obese may also suffer from back pain and degenerative joint diseases such as arthritis.

Numerous mental health problems are also linked to being overfat. In America, there is a social stigma attached to being obese. The overfat are seen as unattractive, inadequate, unhealthy, undisciplined, insecure, depressed, and having poor personalities. They are also perceived as having higher anxiety levels and having lower self-concepts than healthy weight people. These characteristics are certainly not true of everyone who is overfat. Those who find themselves with too much fat, however, are still perceived this way.

Obesity has also been linked to a shorter life span. Research has indicated that those who are moderately overfat may have a 40 percent higher risk of a shortened life span than those whose body fat levels are healthy. Also, severe obesity may result in a 70 percent higher risk of dying early than those with healthy body fat levels.

## THE PROBLEMS WITH DIETING BY ITSELF

Study after study demonstrates that dieting alone does not work for the majority of participants. This is especially true if it is a very low-calorie diet. The multibillion-dollar diet industry wants you to believe that to lose weight and fat, you only need to follow their special diets. Most diets not only fail to deliver on their guarantees, they can also lead to serious health problems such as low blood pressure, heart disease, and sudden death.

Dieting alone may slow the rate of fat loss and may predispose you to a rapid weight gain. Your body interprets dietary restrictions as famine and responds in a defensive manner by slowing its metabolic rate and enhancing its ability to store excess calories as fat. Dieting alone can also tend to use up muscle tissue, considered the body's fat burner. Any loss of muscle mass will lower the body's capacity to burn calories and decrease the chances of losing weight.

Analyze a diet carefully before following it. If you come across a diet that promises you the cake, icing, and candles too, evaluate it using the

Be cautious of diet books.

Liquid diets and diet aids seldom work in the long run.

following criteria. Stay away from any special diets unless you get all "yes" responses from the following questions:

Does it encourage a weight loss of no more than one to two pounds a week?

Does it encourage physical activity?

Does it contain a selection of nutritious foods?

Does it emphasize medium-sized portions?

Does it use foods that are easy to locate and prepare?

Does it give you enough variety?

Can you follow it wherever you eat—at home, work, restaurants, or social events?

Is the cost reasonable?

Can you live on this diet *for the rest of your life?*

## STRATEGIES FOR LIFETIME WEIGHT AND FAT MANAGEMENT

The key to permanent fat management is a new lifestyle approach that is flexible, accepting, and family-based. It discourages calorie counting and food-focused programs that encourage dieting. The act of losing weight and fat poses certain health risks such as cardiovascular disease, high blood pressure, diabetes,

# Fitness Tip

## Create Your Own Motivation

- Think positively. Know you can and will do it. Think about the new you—feeling, looking, and functioning better.
- Use rewards. When you reach a goal, give yourself a compliment ("I did it!"). Buy something special for yourself, too.
- Write down at least five reasons why you want to lose weight and fat. Read them daily.
- Set realistic goals. Experts recommend losing no more than 1 to 2 pounds a week.
- Visualize yourself with your new body six months from now and one year from now.
- Write out a contract. This will raise your level of commitment.

and sleep apnea. Due to these potential dangers, experts strongly recommend a consultation with a physician before and during any program. This new lifestyle program includes five important strategies: (1) Get Psyched!, (2) Get Nutritionally Aware!, (3) Change Unhealthy Behaviors!, (4) Get Physically Active!, and (5) Get Support!

## ▶ Get Psyched!

**Motivation** is the drive or desire to begin or continue a behavior. It is the first step in a lifetime weight and fat control program. Your success, in large part, will be determined by your level of motivation. The more motivated you are, the better your chance of success. If you are self-motivated, you strive to reach your goals for internal rewards. Experts in goal attainment believe internal rewards such as self-esteem and self-confidence are more powerful than external rewards such as money and gifts. Whether you use one type of reward over the other, or combine both, the key is to use whatever works for you.

## ▶ Get Nutritionally Aware!

Eating is one of life's pleasures, so it is important to have a basic understanding of nutrition for making sensible, well-balanced food selections. The same guidelines for good nutrition can be applied to guidelines for lifetime fat

# Fitness Tip

## Use Nutritional Strategies

- Practice variety, balance, and moderation.
- Avoid diets that are less than 1,200 calories for women and 1,500 calories for men.
- Don't skip meals.
- Be aware of the calories in foods. One medium-sized apple equals 76 calories, but one slice of apple pie equals 345 calories.
- If you choose to count calories, follow the 500-calorie deficit rule. Such a deficit will equal a loss of 3,500 calories or 1 pound of stored body fat per week.
- Drink at least eight glasses of water a day.
- Cut out rich desserts. Enjoy fresh fruits instead.
- Always use a shopping list.
- Snack healthy. Serve low-calorie vegetables and fruits.
- Think lean: Trim any visible fat from meat, remove chicken skin before cooking, and use low-fat dairy products. Go easy on the salad dressings, butter, and sour cream.
- Remember, this is a lifetime program of good nutrition and weight/fat control. Conquer one change at a time.

management. These include eating small amounts of fat, saturated fat, cholesterol, sugar, and salt; eating adequate amounts of complex carbohydrates, vegetables, fruits, and fiber; and establishing healthy food relationships.

Reducing dietary fat will eliminate an enormous amount of extra calories and lead to better health. Every gram of fat you consume is equal to nine calories. This is more than double the four calories each in one gram of carbohydrate and in one gram of protein. Plus, the more fat in your diet, the higher your risk of heart disease and some cancers. This is true even if you are not overfat.

Follow the Food Guide Pyramid and use smaller portions. A well-balanced diet is your source of dynamic energy. When losing weight and fat, your body still needs the nutrients and calories necessary for optimal functioning. The Food Guide Pyramid (see figure 9-3 in chapter 9) will serve as a program to follow in choosing nutritious foods. Also, smaller portions of the daily recommended servings are helpful to reduce the number of calories.

# Fitness Tip

## Use Behavioral Strategies

- Keep a food diary to determine eating patterns.
- Satisfy your hunger with vegetables, fruits, and grains before eating fatty foods and sweets.
- Slow down so that your appetite controls how much you eat.
- Eat only when you are physically hungry.
- Plan your meals in advance.
- Concentrate on eating. Avoid watching TV or reading.
- Reinforce your new healthy habits. Give yourself a pat on the back and rewards.
- Learn to relax when eating.
- Substitute other activities for snacking. Take a walk, read, or call a friend.
- Plan for holidays and other special occasions.
- Use smaller plates and chew food slowly.
- Only eat at the table. *Never* eat standing up.
- Use self-discipline. Keep problem food (chips, sweets) out of sight and out of mind.
- Keep nutritious food in sight and in mind.
- Think of food as fuel for the body, instead of simply pleasure for the taste buds.
- If you lapse (overeating, junking out), return to your program—think of it as a learning experience.
- Eat breakfast to decrease the chance of overeating and impulsive snacking.

## ▶ Change Unhealthy Behaviors!

Eating behavior is influenced by physical, emotional, and social factors. Why do you eat? Is it only when you are hungry? When do you eat? Is it only at meal times? Or when you are happy? Sad? Bored? With others? By yourself? In front of the television? While you read? When you drink? When you are upset? Angry? When you celebrate? When you are depressed? Your answers may indicate that your eating patterns are dictated by factors other than hunger. Knowing why you eat and what provokes you to eat will help you improve your eating habits.

# Fitness Tip

## Benefits of Exercise

- **Uses Calories.** Aerobic exercise can be done at a comfortable pace for 30 to 60 minutes. With each minute of activity, you are using up more calories than you would be at rest.
- **Increases Basal Metabolic Rate.** If you do plan to diet, exercise can help keep your BMR up when your body wants to slow it down. After finishing a workout, your metabolic rate is increased for several hours, continuing to use calories at a faster pace.
- **Shrinks Fat Cells.** Exercise can reduce the size of the fat cells. Based on current scientific evidence, it does not appear that you can reduce the number of fat cells. However, you can shrink their size and lower your percent body fat.
- **Prevents Loss of Muscle.** Resistance exercises such as weight training accelerate the rate of muscle buildup and metabolic rate

Modifying or changing your behaviors (behavior modification) is the cornerstone for a program of lifetime weight and fat control. It is built on the idea that all behaviors are learned responses from environmental cues or previous experiences. As you learn to change unhealthy habits (going back for seconds), eating becomes a more conscious act and healthy habits are adopted (eating more slowly).

## ▶ Get Physically Active!

Evidence indicates that obesity is more dependent on inactivity than on overeating. Although we eat fewer calories than Americans did in the early 1900s, we are much fatter. Why? Activity levels have declined significantly. Elevators, riding lawn mowers, power tools, remote controls, and mobile phones are a few examples of how technology has prevented us from using more calories. Due to the sedentary American way of life, it is vital to engage in voluntary physical activity as a strategy for fat loss.

The most significant factor in achieving lifetime weight and fat control is regular, moderate exercise. The American College of Sports Medicine recommends two forms of exercise for fat loss: aerobic exercise and strength-training activities like weight lifting. Aerobic activities such as walking, jogging, bicycling, swimming, dancing, and cross-country skiing are excellent calorie-burning exercises because they are performed continuously for long periods. Resistance training or

**TABLE 10-3**
**Strategies for Controlling Body Fat**

|  | Lower Limit | Upper Limit |
|---|---|---|
| Frequency: | 5 days per week | 7 days per week |
| Intensity: | 60% of maximum heart rate | 80% of maximum heart rate |
| Time: | 30 min. per session | 60 min. per session |
| Type: | Aerobic and resistance training | Aerobic/Anaerobic and resistance training |

Note: Walking is an excellent aerobic activity for controlling body fat because it is low-impact, convenient, and enjoyable.

resistance exercise (weights, sit-ups, push-ups) will help increase muscle tissue, thereby increasing metabolism and using more calories.

To complement the fat-loss effects of aerobic exercise and resistance training, become more active in your leisure time. To give a boost to your fat control program, you can watch less television, drive less, walk more, use stairs, plant a garden, play with the dog, and participate in active sports.

To promote long-term adherence and reduce weight and body fat, follow the **FITT** exercise formula. Many motivated participants, eager to lose weight and fat, start their exercise programs incorrectly by doing too much too soon. The result: another dropout statistic. Follow the exercise guidelines found in table 10-3 for a safe and effective way to reduce body fat.

At the beginning of an exercise program, a loss of inches and body fat will occur, but not necessarily weight. During the first six to eight weeks of your exercise program, you may not lose any weight. Muscle is more dense than fat, so you may experience a slight increase in body weight during this time. However, because the weight gained is muscle and the weight lost is fat, you will be healthier and should experience a decrease in body circumference measurements. Beginning exercisers will often lose inches and have their clothes fit better while remaining at the same weight.

## ▶ Get Support!

Support from family, friends, and groups is an important piece of the weight/fat-control puzzle. No question about it—losing weight and fat is no easy task. The more ammunition you have in your arsenal, the better your chances of success. To improve your odds, enlist the support of family, friends, roommates, and groups. Maybe you can enlist a friend or family member who also wants to lose unwanted pounds and inches. Although the cheering of others can be crucial to your success, the most important support must come from you. With your personal commitment in place, your mission can be accomplished.

# Fitness Tip

## Create a Supportive Environment

- Recruit at least one friend or family member who will stand by you at all times. Make out a contract and have this person sign it.
- Announce your weight and fat control plans to as many people as possible. You will be more committed and will not want to let them down.
- Make a game out of it. For every centimeter (ounce, inch, pound) you lose, you receive a dollar from your support team. If gains occur, you pay.
- Stay in contact with those supporting you. Share your successes. Lean on them during difficult times.
- Plan a celebration event for your success with your support team. Then carry it out after you reach your goals.
- Join a support group.

## RELAPSES

Although **relapses** are common among participants engaging in behavior change, they can serve as learning experiences to build upon for future success. When attempting a health change, it is almost inevitable for most people to relapse and revert back to old, unhealthy habits. The three most common reasons for relapse are: (1) stress-related factors (major life changes, depression, job and school changes, and illness); (2) social factors (traveling, eating out, entertaining); and (3) self-enticing behaviors, such as putting yourself in positions to determine how much you can get away with (e.g., "one bite of ice cream won't hurt me," leading to "I'll just have one scoop," and finally, "I haven't done so well, I might as well eat the whole gallon").

Falling back to old behaviors is part of being human. If you slip back, know why and learn from the experience. Feeling guilt or anger toward yourself for not sticking with it may hinder your efforts. Pick yourself up and get back on track. If you have the will, and blend it with perseverance, you will be successful with your weight and fat goals.

Receiving support from others is important to your weight and fat control.

## MAINTAINING DESIRABLE WEIGHT AND FAT

Once you have arrived at your desirable weight and body fat level, you are halfway there. The challenge now is to achieve weight and fat maintenance for the rest of your life. The solution is a healthy, active lifestyle, including the five keys to lifetime weight and fat control.

## GAINING WEIGHT

Those who need to gain weight can benefit from a change in their eating and exercise patterns. Most people who desire to gain weight want to gain lean body tissue (muscle), not fat tissue. Only those who have body fat percentages below 10 percent for women and 5 percent for men might want to gain additional fat. For weight gain, consume more calories from complex carbohydrates such as pasta, rice, bread, potatoes, and cereals. In addition to a high-carbohydrate diet, regular exercise (including resistance training) can add weight by increasing muscle.

## SUMMARY

- The vast majority of Americans are concerned about their appearance, with body fat being a major issue.
- The weight-loss industry is a multibillion dollar business.
- Sedentary living that also includes overeating, excessive television viewing, movies, and video games contributes to our present condition of unhealthy weight and body fat.
- Many individuals are obsessed with their weight due to America's culture of "thin is in."
- The main reason for managing weight and body fat includes living life to its fullest and enjoying family, school, work, and leisure time.
- Dieting alone does not work.
- The five strategies for lifetime weight and fat management are: 1) Get Psyched!, 2) Get Nutritionally Aware!, 3) Change Unhealthy Behaviors!, 4) Get Physically Active!; and 5) Get Support!
- Relapses can serve as learning experiences to build upon for future success.
- For more information about weight/fat control, go to this address: www.mhhe.com/hper/physed

# Assessment 10-1

Name                              Section              Date

The purpose of this activity is to design your weight and fat management program. Whether you plan to lose, maintain, or gain weight and fat, this contract will be helpful in reaching your goals. See the Fitness Tips in the chapter to answer the questions.

I, _____, commit myself to a weight and fat management program beginning _____, I plan to _____, (lose/gain/maintain) weight and fat, using the five strategies that follow.

## MOTIVATION

What motivational tips do you plan to follow?

1. _____

2. _____

3. _____

4. _____

5. _____

## NUTRITIONAL AWARENESS

What nutritional strategies do you plan to adopt to eat better?

1. _____

2. _____

3. _____

4. _____

5. _____

## BEHAVIOR MODIFICATION

What behavior modification tips do you plan to adopt to develop better eating behaviors?

1. _____

2. _____

3. _____

4. _____

5. _____

## PHYSICAL ACTIVITY

How would you rate your current level of activity: high, medium, or low?
_____

Check these exercise guidelines you plan to follow:

| | | |
|---|---|---|
| Frequency | __ 5 to 7 days a week | _____ |
| Intensity | __ 60 to 80 percent of maximum heart rate | _____ |
| Time | __ 30 to 60 minutes per session | _____ |
| Type | __ Aerobic | _____ |
| Resistance training | __ Add weight training | _____ |
| Start slowly | __ Gradual buildup | _____ |

## SUPPORTIVE ENVIRONMENT

Have your support team (family, friends, and others) write their names on the following lines, signifying their support for your fat control program.

_____

_____

_____

_____

_____

_____

_____

# CHAPTER 11

# STICKING **WITH** IT

## OBJECTIVES

*After reading this chapter, you should be able to do the following:*

- Explain why motivation is the key to exercise adherence.
- Identify and describe your motivation to exercise.
- List at least three motivational strategies that will help you stick with your fitness program.

## KEY TERMS

*While reading this chapter, you will become familiar with the following terms:*

► **Adherence**

► **Goal**

► **Motivation**

► **Strategies**

# Fitness Tip

## Identifying Your Motivation

What is your motivation for walking? If you know the answer to that question, you will be able to develop strategies that will support your goals and keep your motivational level high.

Sticking with an exercise program is the most difficult part for most people. Research and experience indicate that people need more than knowledge to stick with an exercise program. They need motivation.

Walking has a better **adherence** rate than many other exercise programs. However, the dropout rate is still too high. Will you be one who quits, or will you have what it takes to make a commitment and stick with it?

## MOTIVATION

The most significant obstacle to regular exercise is a lack of **motivation.** Many people start exercise programs every year. Why do some stick with it and enjoy the benefits, while others quit and suffer the consequences? Motivation. Those who are highly motivated, and who maintain their motivation, stick with their exercise programs despite the difficulties and obstacles that arise. Those who are not highly motivated are easily defeated by the smallest difficulties and often welcome any excuse to quit.

What motivates human behavior? You can find lists and categories from many different sources. Some of the things that motivate exercise adherence include:

- A sense of control
- A feeling of pride
- A feeling of importance
- A feeling of success
- Recognition
- Approval
- A feeling of achievement
- A feeling of belonging
- Variety
- Movement
- A sense of freedom
- A feeling of self-respect
- Good health (feeling good)
- Appearance (looking good)

What is your motivation to exercise? What do you want from your exercise program? How strong is your motivation to get what you want from your exercise program? These are factors that will determine if you stick with it or quit.

Making a contract is a strategy for sticking with your new behavior.

## MOTIVATIONAL STRATEGIES

Many motivational **strategies** have proven successful for exercise adherence. What works for one person may not, and probably will not, work for another person. Identify your motivation to exercise and select strategies that will help you maintain your motivation.

### ▶ Goals

Setting a **goal** will give you direction and motivation. What do you want from your participation in a fitness walking program? If you have a burning desire to reach your goal you will be motivated to stick with it.

To be effective your goals must be clear, definite, specific, measurable, realistic, believable, and written. Set a reasonable date for the accomplishment of your goal. Start with small goals and in a short time. Success breeds success. As you achieve smaller goals in a shorter time, you will gain confidence in your ability to progressively reach larger goals that take longer.

---

▶ **Adherence**
Steady or faithful attachment.

▶ **Goal**
The end toward which an effort is directed.

▶ **Motivation**
Something that causes a person to act.

▶ **Strategies**
Careful plans directed toward a goal.

# Fitness Tip

## Setting Walking Goals

Set clear and measurable goals that are reasonable for you. If you know exactly what you hope to accomplish, you will have a better chance of success.

▶ **Attitude**

Often the difference between success and failure is attitude. A positive attitude produces positive results. A negative attitude produces negative results. You can program your mind for success. With a positive attitude you will look forward to each walking session. You will enjoy each walk. You will benefit from each walk. You will feel good about yourself during and after each walk.

▶ **Enjoyment**

Enjoyment is important to exercise adherence. If exercise is fun you will want to participate. If you make it miserable you will not want to participate. Different people find exercise enjoyment in different ways. What produces exercise enjoyment for you? Whether you think you will enjoy your walk, or you think you won't, you are right.

▶ **Belief**

Everything in life has a price. To continue any activity, you must believe that the benefits you receive from it are worth the price you pay. To stick with a regular exercise program you must believe that the benefits you receive from it are worth your investment of time, energy, effort, and money. Do you believe in your exercise program? Do you believe it will produce the results you want? Do you believe the results are worth the cost? Regular exercisers have a common belief that exercise is good for them and it is a good investment. What is the value of looking good and feeling good?

▶ **Plan**

Many people are so busy doing that they don't take time to plan what they should be doing. Consequently, they are busy all the time but they are not enjoying life because they are not getting what they really want out of life. Decide what you want out of life and plan your time accordingly. Plan a daily schedule, write it down, and follow it. Plan your exercise program, plan time in your daily and weekly schedule to exercise, write it down, and follow it.

▶ **Priority**

If you value your health, place a high priority on good health habits. Once you decide to include fitness walking in your life, make a commitment. Regular exercise must be important enough to put into your daily and weekly schedule. If you place a high priority on your fitness walking program, you will plan it into your schedule. Don't let less important things interfere with your planned exercise time. Make it a point to exercise at your scheduled time. Most people will come to respect you and admire you for sticking with your exercise commitment, and they will not expect you to be available for anything else at that time. Perhaps more important, you will have more respect for yourself. Regularity is important to the success of your walking program. Reaching worthwhile goals requires dedication, discipline, and persistence.

▶ **Time**

You can't save time you can only spend it. Time passes at the same rate for everyone. Each of us gets 24 hours a day and 168 hours a week. A common excuse for not exercising is "I don't have time to exercise." We all have the same amount of time each day, each week, each month, and each year. On what are you spending your time? What is the most important use of your time? You need to decide what is most important in your life and schedule your time accordingly.

▶ **Action**

One of the most common barriers to success is procrastination. Instead of starting a fitness walking program next year, next month, next week, or tomorrow, start today. Do it now. Change to a healthier lifestyle right now. Make the decision and take action. Take control. Discipline yourself to exercise on a regular basis until it becomes a habit.

▶ **Habit**

It takes at least 21 days for a new behavior to become a habit. After about a month of completing your planned walk at your scheduled time, regular exercise will become a new healthy habit, like brushing your teeth, eating healthy balanced meals, and getting a healthy amount of sleep.

▶ **Reward**

Regular exercisers experience a sense of satisfaction, an intrinsic reward, from regular exercise. It makes them feel good. It is often the best part of their day. It is something they truly enjoy and look forward to. The feeling they get during and after exercise is the reward.

Extrinsic rewards can also be motivating. Reward yourself when you reach one of your exercise goals. Give yourself something special, something you really want. It should be a healthy reward such as a vacation, new walking shoes, new clothes, or a new music CD. Only you know what would be an appropriate motivating reward.

## ▶ Convenience

Many people claim they do not exercise because "it is too inconvenient." To combat this, make your fitness walking program as convenient as possible. The more available your exercise program is to you, the easier it is to stick with it. Identify the factors making your fitness walking program inconvenient for you and begin to resolve them one at a time. The following are some tips to reduce the inconvenience. Place your walking shoes by the door so you don't have to look for them. Keep your walking clothes in the same place so you can find them quickly and easily. Lay out your walking clothes the night before if you plan to walk in the morning. If you plan to walk later in the day, lay out your walking clothes in the morning to remind you and make the transition easier. Schedule your walking time early in the morning when there are fewer conflicting activities, commitments, priorities, and people. These are a few suggestions. Create your solutions to make exercise more convenient for you.

## ▶ Progression

Gradual progression is one of the important principles of effective exercise programs. If you look at the Rockport Walking Programs or the American Heart Association Program in this book you will see that they start off with lower intensity and shorter duration and gradually build to higher intensity and longer duration over a period of weeks and months. Take your time and pace yourself. The greatest benefits of exercise come from a lifetime of regular moderate exercise. Start slowly, enjoy each exercise session, and progress slowly. Gradually increase exercise intensity, duration, and frequency at a rate to which your body can adapt. This will help minimize soreness, bring positive results, and keep your motivation high for a lifelong fitness program.

## ▶ Variety

Boredom is sometimes given as an excuse for quitting an exercise program. Whereas doing the same exercise routine every day appeals to some people, others are easily bored with repetition. Some people enjoy, and find comfort, in routine. They can do the same walk at the same time every day for years and enjoy it. Others are bored if they do the same walk two days in a row.

If you begin to become bored, use your creativity to invent new ways of adding variety to your fitness walking program. The following are some ideas to add variety to your walking program:

- Explore new routes such as parks, golf courses, hiking trails, beaches, new neighborhoods, and so on
- Find new walking friends
- Use earphones to listen to music (be careful around traffic)
- Use different walking speeds
- Walk in the shallow end of a swimming pool or in the ocean
- Walk hills
- Walk stairs
- Walk to complete errands
- Enter walking events

These are only a few ideas. Use your creativity to invent other fun variations. If you begin to get bored with your walking program, change it. In most locations changes in the weather and the seasons create variety. Enjoy each season and each change in the weather.

If you need more variety consider mixing in some other cardiovascular exercise activities; there are many to choose from. To keep things simple, exercise at about the same intensity (heart rate) for about the same length of time. Have fun.

## ▶ Tell Others

If you are starting an exercise program and think you need help to stick with it, tell everyone you know and everyone you meet. Once you make this public commitment it is easier to stick with it. Everyone who knows will ask you how it is going. Each time someone asks it will reinforce your motivation to stick with it.

## ▶ Advantages

Make a list of the advantages and benefits of participating in a regular fitness walking program. If you need help remembering these see chapter 2. This list will help you keep a focus on your reasons to exercise. Whenever you are tempted to skip a workout, look at your list of advantages. This should provide that little extra incentive to put on your walking shoes and take the hardest step of all—the first one.

## ▶ Records

Keep a regular exercise log. Record each fitness walking session. This will provide an account of your progress and achievement. The visual feedback will give you motivation and a sense of accomplishment that will help you stick with your fitness walking program. (See the Walking-for-Fitness Exercise Log in Appendix A.)

There are many ways to chart your progress. Find a level of record keeping that is right for you. Some people just like to put a check mark on a chart or calendar. Others like to keep detailed records of each session's day, date, distance, duration, and exercise heart rate. There are many ways to do this, but somehow

Exercise can be part of your socializing.

give yourself written credit for each completed exercise session. In this way you can visually see your successes accumulate. Soon you will have overwhelming evidence that you can stick with it.

## ▶ Socialize

Walking with others is a strong motivator for some people. It turns fitness walking into a social activity, which can make it more enjoyable. The time can pass quickly when you have someone to talk with. Walking with others can provide safety, companionship, support, and encouragement. Some like to walk with one friend while others like to walk with a group. If you enjoy socializing while exercising, build it into your plan. You are more likely to stick with your fitness walking program when you know someone is counting on you to be at a designated meeting place at a specific time.

## ▶ Clubs

There are many walking clubs. There may already be a club in your area. If not, you might want to start one. The following are some of the things a walking club could do:

- Offer classes
- Teach the benefits of fitness walking
- Teach guidelines for healthy walking programs
- Teach walking techniques
- Provide support and encouragement
- Set up an awards program
- Gain access to indoor facilities
- Conduct fund raising projects
- Arrange trips to special walking events
- Arrange group discounts at local shoe stores

# Fitness Tip

## Make Walking Enjoyable

Your attitude toward walking is important. If you view it as a duty or as punishment, you probably won't continue walking. On the other hand, if you make it fun and view it as something positive you're doing for yourself, walking is more likely to become a lifetime habit.

## ▶ Identity

As you build a history of regular exercise it will become part of your identity. Others will expect you to exercise and you will expect yourself to exercise. Once this happens, sticking with it is easier.

## ▶ Events

You may enjoy participating in special exercise events, such as walking events. You might enjoy this for the competition or for the recognition or for the opportunity to be with others who have similar values and beliefs about exercise.

## ▶ Modify

As the weeks, months, and years pass, change will occur. Your needs, interests, fitness level, living conditions, the weather, and the availability of exercise facilities will change. As these changes take place, you will need to evaluate your fitness walking program periodically to determine if it is still providing the appropriate amount of exercise. The key is to maintain a program that meets your current fitness needs and interests.

Motivational strategies play an important role in sticking with your fitness walking program. Experiment with different ideas and find ones that work best for you. Refer to this chapter anytime you need a dose of encouragement or a shot of motivation. Keep in mind that the most important health and fitness benefits come from a regular, moderate, lifelong program.

## SUMMARY

- Motivation is the key to exercise adherence.
- Goal setting will give you motivation and direction.
- Maintaining a positive attitude toward your fitness walking program is critical to your success.
- Enjoyment is important to exercise adherence.
- Plan your fitness walking program, schedule time for walking, and stick to your plan.
- Evaluate and modify your walking program periodically to make sure it is designed to help you reach your exercise goals.

# Assessment 11-1

_____     _____     _____
Name                        Section         Date

The purpose of this activity is to help you set priorities and identify those things that are most important to you.

List the 10 most important things in your life. After you have written them down, rank them from 1 to 10 (1 being the most important).

**Rank**

_____  _____

_____  _____

_____  _____

_____  _____

_____  _____

_____  _____

_____  _____

_____  _____

_____  _____

_____  _____

1. Does fitness walking contribute to any of the 10 most important things in your life right now?

   Yes    No
   ☐      ☐

2. If your answer is "yes," how high was the ranking of the item(s)?

**175**

# Assessment 11-2

## Identifying Advantages of a Fitness Walking Program

Name _____  Section _____  Date _____

The purpose of this activity is to list the advantages and benefits of participating in a fitness walking program. List the advantages and benefits to be gained by regular participation in a fitness walking program. Refer to Chapters 2, 10, and 12.

Post this list where you will see it every day. If you feel like skipping a workout, look at this list.

This should encourage you to stick with your workout plan.

**Advantages and benefits**

_____

_____

_____

_____

_____

_____

_____

_____

_____

_____

_____

_____

# Assessment 11-3

Name        Section      Date

The purpose of this activity is to identify motivational strategies that will help you stick with your fitness walking program.

Place a check by the motivational strategies you believe will help you stick with your fitness walking program. Once you have selected these strategies, try each one. Then incorporate into your fitness walking program the strategies that work best for you.

_____ Goals

_____ Attitude

_____ Enjoyment

_____ Belief

_____ Plan

_____ Priority

_____ Time

_____ Action

_____ Habit

_____ Reward

_____ Convenience

_____ Progression

_____ Variety

What strategies work best for you?

# Assessment 11-4

## Fitness Walking Contract

Name                                    Section          Date

    The purpose of this activity is to fill out a fitness walking contract, which will affirm your commitment to reach the goals you have set.

    Once you have clearly defined your goals, fill in the contract.

    I, _____, will commit myself to following a fitness walking program.

    The specific goals of my walking program are:

1.
2.
3.

    The specific date(s) I expect to reach my goal(s) is(are):

    Other important reasons I have committed myself to a fitness walking program are:

1.
2.
3.

    Motivational strategies to follow that will help me stay with my fitness walking program are:

1.
2.
3.

    Support people who will help me with my fitness walking program are:

1.
2.
3.

    When I reach my goals, I will reward myself with the following:

Signature _____    Date _____
Witness _____    Witness _____

# WELLNESS THROUGH **HEALTHY** LIFESTYLES

## OBJECTIVES

*After reading this chapter, you should be able to do the following:*

- Define health and wellness.
- Interpret the importance of the wellness-illness continuum.
- Identify and describe the health and wellness components.
- Discuss the importance of lifestyle to wellness.
- Adopt the strategies for well-being.
- Explain the significance of prevention to wellness.

### KEY TERMS

*While reading this chapter, you will become familiar with the following terms:*

- ► Environmental
- ► Health
- ► Lifestyle
- ► Optimal Health

- ► Physical
- ► Prevention
- ► Psychological
- ► Social

*Continued*

## KEY TERMS

*Continued from p. 183*

▶ **Spiritual**                    ▶ **Wellness**

▶ **Vocational**

Every day we make choices that can either enhance or detract from our present state of well-being. Although everyone desires a healthy, quality life, not everyone is willing to make the lifestyle changes necessary to bring about health improvement. However, you may be among the growing number of individuals striving for this richer style of life. This growth in numbers can be attributed to research findings that indicate positive lifestyle behaviors can have a significant influence on our health, quality of life, and well-being.

A choice of pathways lies before you. While many different paths can guide you toward better health and a richer, quality life, only *you* can choose which path to take and at what speed you will travel. Choose wisely, and enjoy your journey.

## HEALTH AND WELLNESS

**Health** is a multifaceted, dynamic quality that describes how well you are able to function at any particular time. Being healthy is much more than not being sick. Your health is made up of psychological, spiritual, physical, social, vocational, and environmental resources that allow you to live a satisfying and productive life. **Optimal health** indicates a high level of functioning and is often characterized by vitality, a zest for life, and a sense of harmony with nature and humanity.

Health is a constantly changing quality in our lives. Our health can be different from day to day and week to week due to changes in our minds, bodies, values, attitudes, beliefs, habits, and behaviors. One example of how our health can change is depicted by Janie, a healthy, active college sophomore. Her uncertainty about what major to declare led to excessive worrying, and eventually, to a preulcer condition. Once Janie declared a major in her junior year, she stopped worrying, her health improved, and she was better able to live her life to the fullest.

**Wellness** includes an enjoyable and positive approach to a lifestyle that promotes a high level of well-being. It is a conscious commitment to growth and improvement in all areas of your life. The focus is on self-responsibility, self-fulfillment, and a richer quality of life. The wellness concept is based on the premise that adopting health-enhancing behaviors will help reduce potential disease risk factors and promote well-being. Table 12-1 highlights the benefits of achieving optimal health.

Health and wellness are closely related. Here is an example of how closely they work together: Having a disease (illness) is like a person walking backward; not being sick but not being well (neutral) is like a person standing still; and being generally healthy is like a person walking forward. When all your behaviors are health-enhancing, you are walking briskly toward optimal health (wellness).

The wellness-illness continuum (see figure 12-1) shows that wellness, or optimal health, is the highest level of functioning possible. The other end of the continuum represents the complete loss of functioning, or death. Where are you now? Place a dot where you stand on the continuum today. Place another dot on the continuum where you were five years ago. Which direction is your lifestyle taking you? Are your choices leading you toward a healthier and more abundant life?

---

► **Health**

A multifaceted, dynamic quality that describes how well you are able to function at any time. It is made up of psychological, spiritual, physical, social, vocational, and environmental resources.

► **Optimal Health**

Indicates a high level of functioning and is often characterized by vitality, a zest for life, and a sense of harmony with nature and humanity.

► **Wellness**

Includes an enjoyable and positive approach to a lifestyle that promotes a high level of well-being.

► **Psychological**

A dynamic process that combines emotional and mental states leading to optimal health.

► **Spiritual**

A positive sense of whatever provides meaning and purpose in your life.

► **Physical**

Achieving optimal health through behaviors such as physical fitness, eating healthy, adequate sleep and rest, and responsible sexual behavior and drug use.

► **Social**

Includes having satisfying, trusting relationships and interacting well with others.

► **Vocational**

Achieving optimal health through finding meaning in and satisfaction with your school, job, and leisure pursuits.

► **Environmental**

The impact the natural world has on health.

► **Lifestyle**

The way an individual chooses to live.

► **Prevention**

To keep from happening.

**TABLE 12-1**
**Major Benefits of Achieving Optimal Health**

1. More "life to your years" (richer quality)
2. More "years to your life" (increased longevity)
3. A healthier mind, body, and spirit
4. Increased self-esteem and confidence
5. Greater zest for life with higher energy levels
6. More humor (fun and playfulness)
7. A positive attitude
8. Less risk for major diseases
9. Stronger immune system to ward off infections
10. More self-control and less reliance on others
11. Lower health-care costs
12. Stronger relationships
13. Improved environmental sensitivity
14. More enjoyment of your roles in life (as student, employee, etc.)
15. Better possibility of achieving your full potential in life
16. Better able to enjoy life's "moments" and experiences

| | |
|---|---|
| *I have never felt better* | Optimal Health (Wellness) |
| *I feel great* | Excellent Health |
| *I feel good* | Good Health |
| *I feel fine* | Above-Average Health |
| *I feel OK* | Neutral |
| *I don't feel so good* | Minor Illness |
| *I feel rotten* | Major Illness |
| *I have never felt worse* | Critical Illness |
| | Death |

**FIGURE 12-1** The wellness-illness continuum.

# HEALTH AND WELLNESS COMPONENTS

To enjoy a healthy lifestyle, many wellness components must work closely together. Your position on the wellness-illness continuum in large part depends on the daily health choices you make. It is influenced by your degree of health in each of the following wellness components: psychological, spiritual, physical, social, vocational, and environmental. The achievement of optimal health is related to being well in each of the six dimensions that follow (figure 12-2).

## ▶ Psychological

**Psychological** well-being combines your emotional and mental states. It is not a static condition but a dynamic process that can change from day to day.

We all have our good days, our bad days, and our okay days. No one has total control over their emotional states (joy, sadness, fear, anger, shyness, loneliness, and guilt). However, emotionally healthy people strive to maintain psychological balance and know when to express their emotions appropriately and comfortably. They are also capable of showing respect and affection for others. In the event of emotional instability, they are willing to join a support group and/or to seek professional help.

**FIGURE 12-2** Health and wellness components.

If you have mental well-being, you can embrace reality for what it is, respond positively to life's changes, and use healthy coping skills to deal with stress and personal problems. Also, you believe in lifelong learning. To fulfill your intellectual needs, you keep your mind active and curious, striving to learn from all of life's experiences.

## ▶ Spiritual

**Spiritual** well-being is a positive sense of whatever provides meaning and purpose in your life. You can use your religion, philosophy, beliefs, values, faith, creed, principles, morals, or ethics to describe it. Knowing your purpose in life and being more comfortable expressing love, joy, peace, and fulfillment are part of spiritual well-being, which also includes helping yourself and others to achieve maximum potential.

Spiritual health also fosters a feeling of being connected with your inner self, significant others, and the universe. Finally, your spirituality includes having hope after setbacks as well as the appreciation of nature.

## ▶ Physical

**Physical** well-being includes being physically fit, eating nutritiously, and getting adequate rest and sleep. Responsible sexual behavior and drug and alcohol use are important to this wellness component. Physical wellness includes a personal awareness and care of the physical self, which involves regular self-tests, checkups, injury and disease rehabilitation, proper use of medications, and taking the appropriate steps when illness does occur.

## ▶ Social

**Social** well-being means having satisfying, trusting relationships and interacting well with others. It includes exhibiting fairness, justice, and concern toward and appreciation of the differences in all people. The idea of being well socially suggests having a network of family members, friends, and others who can be called upon during times of need. A socially well person also feels "connected" with their community.

## ▶ Vocational

**Vocational** well-being is finding meaning in and satisfaction with your school, job, and leisure pursuits. Ask yourself if what you are doing right now in life is stimulating, challenging, and rewarding? If it is, you have a high level of vocational well-being. If it is not, you may want to consider making a change and seeking further training in an area of personal interest. The vocational component includes working in harmony with others to accomplish goals.

Happiness is a welcome emotion.

## ▶ Environmental

Human survival is dependent upon air, water, and land resources. **Environmental** well-being refers to the impact that this natural world has on your health. It includes protecting yourself from hazards, such as secondhand smoke, an example of air pollution that can seriously affect your health. This component also includes being environmentally sensitive—working to preserve Earth through the four Rs: reducing, reusing, recycling, and responsibility.

## IMPORTANCE OF LIFESTYLE TO WELLNESS

Your **lifestyle** (the way you live your life) plays a key role in wellness. Your health habits are the core of your lifestyle. The health choices you make will lead toward health or illness. The effects of these daily decisions are compounded over time—day by day, week by week, month by month, and year by year. The accumulation of positive choices such as fitness walking can lead you toward optimal health and a quality life. The accumulation of negative choices can lead you toward suffering, disease, and premature death.

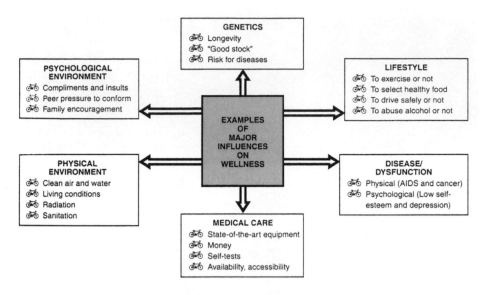

**FIGURE 12-3** Major influences on wellness.

There are other major influences besides lifestyle that influence our health. These are genetics, disease/dysfunction, access to medical care, physical environment, and psychosocial environment. Though all are critical to wellness, most health experts rank lifestyle as the most significant that you have control over. Figure 12-3 provides examples of the major influences on wellness.

Many people begin living a healthy lifestyle only after they have been diagnosed with a disease (cancer, heart disease, diabetes). Fortunately, many of these individuals are able to reverse their illness and restore their health by engaging in the positive lifestyle behavior changes ordered by their physician. Unfortunately, for many others, the damage within the body may be irreversible, leading to premature death.

## STRATEGIES FOR WELL-BEING

To achieve a healthy lifestyle, consider adopting these eight important strategies.

### ▶ 1. Be Accountable

No one else is as responsible for your health as you are—not your physician, parents, friends, or partner. If you believe that health choices are mostly within your control, you are more likely to adopt positive lifestyle changes.

## ▶ 2. Keep a Positive Attitude

An important strategy for well-being is to keep a positive attitude toward yourself, your health, and life in general. When you keep life positive, life has a way of keeping you positive. The following piece of prose by Charles Swindol can empower you to accept responsibility for your attitudes throughout life:

> The longer I live, the more I realize the impact of attitude on life. Attitude to me is more important than facts. It is more important than the past, than education, than money, than circumstances, than failures, than successes, than what other people think or say or do. It is more important than appearance, giftedness, or skill. . . . The remarkable thing is we have a choice every day regarding the attitude we will embrace for that day. We cannot change our past. We cannot change the fact that people will act in a certain way. We cannot change the inevitable. The only thing we can do is play on the one string we have, and that is our attitude. I am convinced that life is 10% what happens to me and 90% how I react to it. As so it is with you . . . we are in charge of our attitudes.

## ▶ 3. Make Lifestyle Changes

What good is health knowledge or having positive attitudes and values if you don't apply it to life? Knowing the importance of exercise and having good intentions to be fit are admirable. However, if you don't act on this wisdom and desire, what have you accomplished? By making positive lifestyle changes, you are more likely to enjoy a high level of wellness.

## ▶ 4. Strive for Balance

A moderate degree of health in the six wellness components is more desirable than being strong in some and weak in others. For example, people who abuse alcohol and drugs at nightly parties may have strong social ties but are also damaging their physical health. A healthy, balanced individual can enjoy all facets of life, including school, work, family, friends, socials, and leisure time.

## ▶ 5. Engage in Variety

Variety is the spice of life and well-being. Staying with the same routine, physical activities, and health foods can lead to boredom and apathy. Consequently, enjoy the variety of all that life has to offer by engaging in many different activities. This type of lifestyle will promote fun and help prevent burnout.

## ▶ 6. Practice Moderation

Any enjoyable behavior performed to excess can lead to burnout and health problems. For example, too much exercise can lead to mental fatigue and injuries. Overindulgence, even of nutritious food, can lead to excess calories and

# Fitness Tip

## Focus on One Change

- Health experts recommend making only one lifestyle change at a time.
- It takes about three weeks for a new behavior to become a normal part of your everyday routine.

weight gain. Positive lifestyle behaviors done in moderation can keep life exciting and fun without creating unnecessary health risks.

## ▶ 7. Take Yourself and Life Lightly

Where is it written that life should always be serious and predictable? Humor (joke telling, playfulness, silliness) has been identified as the miracle drug with only funny side effects. A healthy dose of daily humor and laughter can add joy and playfulness to daily living. Humor and laughter can exercise your heart muscle; improve circulation; increase alertness; and diminish tension, stress, fear, and depression. A sense of humor can facilitate your relationships by enhancing communication skills.

## ▶ 8. Have It Your Way!

It's your life and your health. You are the owner of your mind and body, so you get to make your health decisions. You will have your unique wellness program tailored best to meet your health needs and interests. Once you commit to the decision that your health is a top priority, you will make everyday choices that can help prevent disease and promote well-being.

## PREVENTION AND WELLNESS

An ounce of **prevention** is worth much more than a pound of cure. Imagine you are the owner of a prized dog. To keep her healthy, you will want to give her the best preventive care possible: lots of love and attention; the right amount of exercise and play; a special diet high in nutrients; the proper sleep and rest; and a positive, supportive environment. With this royal treatment, she is sure to enjoy a great, long life. Well, the same can be said for you. You also deserve the best care so that you too can enjoy all that life has to offer. Performing at your full potential can lead to greater happiness, fulfillment, and a richer quality of life.

The time to strive for a high level of wellness is now. Why? First, the earlier that health-enhancing behaviors are adopted, the easier they are to maintain throughout life. Second, the longer a person puts off living a healthy lifestyle, the greater the risk of serious disease. So, if you're ready to add *life to your years* and *years to your life* start now!

## SUMMARY

- Everyday you make choices that will either enhance or detract from your health.
- A growing body of research indicates positive lifestyle behaviors can have a significant influence on your health, quality of life, and well-being.
- The focus of wellness is on self-responsibility, self-fulfillment, and a richer quality of life.
- To enjoy the benefits of a healthy lifestyle, the following six health and wellness components must be addressed: psychological, spiritual, physical, social, vocational, and environmental.
- Your lifestyle is one area you have control over that plays a key role in your wellness.
- Be accountable; be positive; make lifestyle changes; strive for balance, variety, and moderation; take yourself and life lightly; and have it your way. These are strategies to follow for health.
- Practicing disease prevention and health promotion behaviors can lead to performing at your full potential and "add life to your years and years to your life."
- The time to strive for a high level of wellness is now!
- For more information on wellness through healthy lifestyles, go to www.mhhe.com/hper/physed

# Assesment 12-1

## Assessing Your Current Level of Wellness

Name                                    Section                    Date

    The purpose of this activity is to assess your current level of wellness in the six dimensions.

    Review the six wellness components found in chapter 12. On the Wellness Wheel below, place a dot on each line that best represents where you feel you are now. Dots placed close to the inner circle (hub) represent a lower level of health, whereas dots placed near the outer circle (rim) indicate a higher level of health. Next, connect the dots.

Wellness Wheel shows the six dimensions of wellness.

# RESULTS

First—How balanced is your development?

_____

_____

_____

Second—Are you close to achieving a high level of health in each dimension?

_____

_____

What are your strengths? What are your weaknesses?

|  | **Strengths** | **Weaknesses** |
|---|---|---|
| 1. | _____ | _____ |
| 2. | _____ | _____ |
| 3. | _____ | _____ |
| 4. | _____ | _____ |
| 5. | _____ | _____ |
| 6. | _____ | _____ |
| 7. | _____ | _____ |
| 8. | _____ | _____ |

Third—What behaviors can you eliminate, modify, or adopt to improve your health?

Eliminate: _____

Modify: _____

Adopt: _____

_____

# Assessment 12-2

_____    _____    _____
Name                                    Section            Date

    The purpose of this activity is to help you identify lifestyle behaviors that are enhancing or harming your health.

    Place a check in the positive or negative column for each lifestyle behavior. A check in the positive column indicates this behavior is either enhancing your health or not harming your health. A check in the negative column indicates this behavior may be harming your health.

## LIFESTYLE BEHAVIOR

| Do you | Yes | No |
|---|---|---|
| Refrain from using tobacco (including smokeless tobacco) | ____ | ____ |
| Avoid smoke-filled environments | ____ | ____ |
| Avoid use of alcohol in excess | ____ | ____ |
| Maintain a healthy body weight | ____ | ____ |
| Maintain a healthy percent of body fat | ____ | ____ |
| Maintain healthy blood pressure | ____ | ____ |
| Receive adequate amounts of sleep and rest | ____ | ____ |
| Maintain a regular exercise program | ____ | ____ |
| Practice stress management techniques | ____ | ____ |
| Eat breakfast | ____ | ____ |
| Maintain a well-balanced diet | ____ | ____ |
| Consume six daily servings of grains | ____ | ____ |
| Consume three servings of vegetables daily | ____ | ____ |
| Consume two servings of fruits daily | ____ | ____ |
| Limit salt intake | ____ | ____ |
| Limit sugar intake | ____ | ____ |
| Limit fat intake | ____ | ____ |

Wear seat belts regularly                                               _____  _____

Refrain from drinking and driving                                       _____  _____

Receive regular physical examinations                                   _____  _____

Receive regular dental examinations                                     _____  _____

Perform monthly self-exam for lumps/thickening of the skin              _____  _____

Practice abstinence or safe sex                                         _____  _____

Maintain positive attitude toward life                                  _____  _____

Avoid the use of illegal drugs                                          _____  _____

Total                                                                   _____  _____

Add up the positive behaviors and the negative behaviors and place in the total column. Are you satisfied with your results? _____

_____

_____

What are your healthy lifestyle behaviors? _____

_____

_____

What are your unhealthy lifestyle behaviors? _____

_____

_____

What are your strategies to improve the lifestyle behaviors that are taking away from your health?_____

_____

_____

What do your answers tell you? _____

_____

_____

_____

# Appendix A

Name _____

| Day | Date | Distance | Duration | Heart rate |
|-----|------|----------|----------|------------|
|  |  |  |  |  |
|  |  |  |  |  |
|  |  |  |  |  |
|  |  |  |  |  |
|  |  |  |  |  |
|  |  |  |  |  |
|  |  |  |  |  |
|  |  |  |  |  |
|  |  |  |  |  |
|  |  |  |  |  |
|  |  |  |  |  |
|  |  |  |  |  |
|  |  |  |  |  |
|  |  |  |  |  |
|  |  |  |  |  |
|  |  |  |  |  |
|  |  |  |  |  |
|  |  |  |  |  |
|  |  |  |  |  |
|  |  |  |  |  |
|  |  |  |  |  |

# Appendix B

## Information

The Rockport Company
72 Howe St.
Marlboro, MA 01752
www.rockport.com
1-800-762-5767

## Periodicals

The Walking Magazine
P.O. Box 52341
Boulder, CO 80321-2341
www.walkingmag.com

The Atlantic Trailmaster Magazine
6904 Beech Ave.
Baltimore, MD 21206-1200

Walking! Journal
Box 454
Athens, GA 30603

Heart and Sole Newsletter
National Organization of Mall
   Walkers
P.O. Box 191
Hermann, MO 65041

WalkWays
WalkWays Center
733 15th St., NW
Washington, DC 20025

## Walking Tapes

Hooked On Walking
P.O. Box 885
Cypress, TX 77429

Fitness Walking
Arena Marketing
P.O. Box 32080
Kansas City, MO 76411

Happy Walking Tapes
Happy Heart Productions Inc.
Box 1015
Ballwin, MO 63011-9998

Sports Music, Inc.
Box 769689
Roswell, GA 30076
www.sportsmusic.com
1-800-878-4764

Rhythm Walking Tapes
K-Tel
P.O. Box 46004
Minneapolis, MN 55446-9004

Music to Walk By
WalkUSA
6310 Nancy Ridge Road
Ste. 101
San Diego, CA 92121-3209

Walking Tapes
Box 767364
Roswell, GA 30076

## Walking Equipment

WalkUSA
1-800-255-6422

The Sportsvilla
Box 209
Vandalia, MO 63382

PermaID
P.O. Box 400
Columbia, MD 21045

Creative Health Products, Inc.
1000 Saddle Ridge Rd.
Plymouth, MI 48170

## Walking Organizations

American Volkssport Association
Suite 101
Phoenix Square 1001
Pat Booker Road
Universal City, TX 78148

Hot Line 1-800-830-WALK

National Association of Mall Walkers
P.O. Box 191
Hermann, MO 65041

International Walking Society
P.O. Box 4037
Boulder, CO 80306

Walking Association
655 Rancho Catalina Place
Tucson, AZ 86704

Walking World Institute
P.O. Box K Gracie Station
New York, NY 10028
(212) 988-8319

## Walking Tours

Country Walkers
P.O. Box 180 W
Waterbury, VT 05676

Progressive Trails, Inc.
1932 1st Ave., Ste. 1100-W
Seattle, WA 98101

Distant Journeys
P.O. Box 1211
Camden, ME 04843

Roads Less Traveled
P.O. Box 18742-K3
Boulder, CO 80308

# References and Suggested Readings

Allsen, P. E., Harrison, J. M., & Vance, B. (1997). *Fitness for Life: An Individualized Approach.* 6th ed. New York: McGraw-Hill.

Alter, M. J. (1996). *Science of Flexibility.* 2d ed. Champaign, IL: Human Kinetics.

American Cancer Society. *Cancer Facts and Figures.* Atlanta, GA: American Cancer Society, 1996.

————. *The Smoke Around You: The Risks of Involuntary Smoking.* Atlanta, GA: American Cancer Society, 1995.

————. *Taking Control: 10 Steps to a Healthier Life and Reduced Cancer Risk.* Atlanta, GA: American Cancer Society, 1992.

American College of Sports Medicine. *Guidelines for Graded Exercise Testing and Exercise Prescription.* 5th ed. Philadelphia: Lea & Febiger, 1995.

————. *The American Heart Association Diet: An Eating Plan for Healthy Americans.* Dallas, TX: American Heart Association, 1993.

————. *1996 Heart and Stroke Facts.* Dallas, TX: American Heart Association, 1995.

Anderson, B. (1980). *Stretching.* Bolinas, CA: Shelter.

Anspaugh, D. J., Hamrick, M. H., & Rosato, F. D. (2001). *Wellness: Concepts and Applications.* 4th ed. New York: Mcgraw-Hill.

Ardell, D. B., & Tager, M. J. (1988). *Planning for Wellness: A Guidebook for Achieving Optimal Health.* 3d ed. Dubuque, IA: Kendall/Hunt.

Brody, J. "Walking for Fitness," *Corpus Christi (Texas) Caller Times,* 20 May 1966, pp. 6–7.

Brooks, G. A., & Fahey, T. D. (1987). *Fundamentals of Human Performance.* New York: Macmillan.

Brown, H. L. (1992). *Lifetime Fitness.* 3d ed. Scottsdale, AZ: Gorsuch Scarisbrick.

Cairns, M. (1985). Racewalking—A Fitness Alternative. *Journal of Physical Education, Recreation, and Dance,* 50–51.

Callaway, C. W. (1988). Biological Adaptations to Starvation and Semistarvation. In R. T. Frankie & M. Yang (Eds.), *Obesity and Weight Control.* Rockville, MD: Aspen.

Campbell, K. R., Adres, R., Greer, N. L., Hintermeister, R., & Rippe, J. (1987). The Effects of Fatigue on Selected Biomechanical Parameters in Fitness Walking. *Medicine and Science in Sports and Exercise,* 19, 518.

Coleman, R. J., Wilkie, S., Viscio, L., O'Hanley, S., Porcari, J., Kline, G., Keller, B., Hsieh, S., Freedson, P. S., & Rippe, J. (1987). Validation of a One-Mile Test for Estimating $\dot{V}O_2$max in 20–29 Year Olds. *Medicine and Science in Sports and Exercise,* 19, 528.

Concepts of Physical Fitness. *www.mhhe.com/hper/physed/clw/student*

Cooper, K. H. (1968). *Aerobics.* New York: Bantam.

Cooper, K. H. (1970). *The New Aerobics.* New York: Bantam.

Cooper, K. H. (1977). *The Aerobics Way.* New York: Bantam.

Cooper, K. H. (1982). *The Aerobics Program for Total Well-Being: Exercise, Diet, Emotional Balance.* New York: Bantam.

Cooper, M., & Cooper, K. H. (1972). *Aerobics for Women.* New York: Bantam.

Corbin, C. B., Lindsey, R., & Welk, C. J. (2000). *Concepts of Physical Fitness: Active Lifestyles for Wellness.* 10th ed. New York: McGraw-Hill.

Corbin, D. E. (1988). *Jogging.* Glenview, IL: Scott, Foresman.

Couey, R. B. (1982). *Building God's Temple.* Minneapolis: Burgess.

DeBenedette, V. (August 1988). Keeping Pace with the Many Forms of Walking. *The Physician and Sportsmedicine* 16(8): 145–150.

Dietary Guidelines For Americans, 2000, 5th Edition, USDA. www.nal.usda.gov/fnic/dga/index.html

DiGennaro, J. (1983). *The New Fitness: Exercise for Everybody.* Englewood, CO: Morton.

Dishman, R. K. (Ed.). (1988). *Exercise Adherence: Its Impact on Public Health.* Champaign, IL: Human Kinetics.

Fahey, T. D. (2000). *Super Fitness for Sports, Conditioning, and Health.* Boston, MA: Allyn & Bacon.

Feeney, P. (Ed.). (1990). *What's in a Label? A Dietitian's Handbook for Helping Consumers Demystify Food Labels.* American Dietetic Association and ConAgra. Chicago, IL.

Friedman, R. M. (Ed.). (October 1988). Fatter Calories. *University of California, Berkeley Wellness Letter,* 5, 1–2.

Greer, N., Campbell, K., Andres, R., Hintermeister, R., & Rippe, J. (1987). An Evaluation of Walking and Running Shoes During Walking. *Medicine and Science in Sports and Exercise,* 19, 517.

Greer, N. L., Campbell, K. R., Foley, P. M., Andres, R. O., & Rippe, J. M. (1986). An Assessment of the Reliability of Ground Reaction Forces During Walking. *Medicine and Science in Sports and Exercise,* 18, S81.

Hales, D. (2001). *An Invitation to Health.* 9th ed. Redwood City, CA: Benjamin/Cummings.

Hawkins, J. D., & Hawkins, S. M. (2001). *Walking for Fun and Fitness.* 3d ed. Belmont, CA: Wadsworth/Thomson.

Healthy People 2010. *http://web.health.gov/healthypeople*

Henderson, J. (1988). *Total Fitness: Training for Life.* Dubuque, IA: Wm. C. Brown.

Hesson, J. L. (2000). *Weight Training for Life.* 5th ed. Belmont, CA: Wadsworth/Thomson.

Hoeger, W. W., & Hoeger, S. A. (2001). *Fitness and Wellness.* 5th ed. Belmont, CA: Wadsworth/Thomson.

Iknoian, Therese. (1995). *Fitness Walking.* Champaign, IL: Human Kinetics.

Jonas, S., & Radetsky, P. (1988). *PaceWalking: The Balanced Way to Aerobic Health.* New York: Crown.

Kashlwa, A., & Rippe, J. (1987). *Fitness Walking for Women.* New York: Putnam.

Katch, F. I., & McArdle, W. D. (1983). *Nutrition, Weight Control and Exercise.* 2d ed. Philadelphia: Lea and Febiger.

Keesey, R. E. (1986). A Set-Point Theory of Obesity. In K. D. Brownell & J. P. Foreyt (Eds.), *Handbook of Eating Disorders.* New York: Basic.

Kemper, D. K., Giuffre, J., & Drabinski, G. (1985). *Pathways: A Successful Guide for a Healthy Life.* Boise, ID: Healthwise.

Kline, G., Porcari, J., Freedson, P., Ward, A., Ross, J., Wilkie, S., & Rippe, J. (1987). Does Aerobic Capacity Affect the Validity of the One Mile Walk $VO_2$max Prediction? *Medicine and Science in Sports and Exercise,* 19, 528.

Kline, G., Porcari, J., Hintermeister, R., Freedson, P., McCarron, R., Rippe, J., Ross, J., Ward, A., & Gurry, M. (1986). Prediction of $VO_2$max from a One-Mile Track Walk. *Medicine and Science in Sports and Exercise,* 18, S35.

Kline, G. M., Porcari, J.P., Hintermeister, R., Freedson, P. S., Ward, A., McCarron, R. F., Ross, J., & Rippe, J. M. (1987). Prediction of $VO_2$max from a One-Mile Track Walk. *Medicine and Science in Sports and Exercise,* 19, 253.

Koszuta, L. E. (August/September 1988). Splash On By. *The Walking Magazine,* Vol. 4, 65–70.

Kuntzleman, C. T., & Editors of Consumer Guide. (1978). *The Complete Book of Walking.* New York: Simon and Schuster.

Levy, M. R., Dignan, M., & Shirreffs, J. H. (1992). *Life and Health: Targeting Wellness.* New York: McGraw-Hill.

Makalous, S. L., Arauj, M. A., & Thomas, T. R. (April 1988). Energy Expenditure during Walking with Hand Weights. *The Physician and Sportsmedicine,* 16(4): 139–148.

Mayer, J. (1975) An Hour of Exercise vs. a Pound of Flesh. In B. Q. Hafen (Ed.), *Overweight and Obesity: Causes, Fallacies, Treatment.* Provo, UT: Brigham Young University Press.

McCarron, R., Kline, G., Freedson, P., Ward, A., & Rippe, J. (1986). Fast Walking Is an Adequate Aerobic Stimulus for High Fit Males. *Medicine and Science in Sports and Exercise,* 18, S21.

McGlynn, G. (1999). *Dynamics of Fitness: A Practical Approach.* 5th ed. New York: McGraw-Hill.

Melograno, V. J., & Klinzing, J. E. (1988). *An Orientation to Total Fitness.* 4th ed. Dubuque, IA: Kendall/Hunt.

Miller, D. K., & Allen, T. E. (1986). *Fitness: A Lifetime Commitment.* 3d ed. Edina, MN: Burgess.

Montoye, H. J., Christian, J. L., Nagle, F. J., & Levin, S. M. (1988). *Living Fit.* Menlo Park, CA: Benjamin/Cummings.

Nestle Worldview. (Spring 1992). *Maintaining a Healthy Weight* (Vol. 4, No. 1). Washington, DC: Nestle Information Service.

Nestle Worldview. (Spring 1992). *Weighing the Facts on Obesity* (Vol. 4, No. 1). Washington, DC: Nestle Information Service.

Nestle Worldview. (Winter 1992) *Vitamins: Building Blocks of Better Health* (Vol. 3, No. 4). Washington, DC: Nestle Information Service.

O'Hanley, S., Ward, A., Zwiren, L., McCarron, R., Ross, J., & Rippe, J. M. (1987). Validation of a One-Mile Walk Test in 70–79 Year-Olds. *Medicine and Science in Sports and Exercise,* 19, 528.

Porcari, J., Kline, G., Hintermeister, R., Freedson, P., Ward, A., Gurry, M., Ross, J., McCarron, R., & Rippe, J. (1986). Is Fast Walking an Adequate Aerobic Training Stimulus? *Medicine and Science in Sports and Exercise,* 18, S81.

Porcari, J., McCarron, R., Kline, G., Freedson, P., Ward, A., Ross, J., & Rippe, J. (1987). Is Fast Walking an Adequate Aerobic Training Stimulus in 30–69 Year Old Adults? *The Physician and Sports Medicine,* 15, 119.

Powers, Scott K. & Dodd, Scott K. *Total Fitness: Exercise, Nutrition, and Wellness.* 2d ed. (1999). Boston, MA: Allyn & Bacon.

Prentice, W. E. (2001). *Get Fit, Stay Fit.* 2d ed. New York: McGraw Hill.

Pruitt, B. E., & Stein, J. J. (1999). *Healthstyles: Decisions for Living Well.* 2d ed. Boston, MA: Allyn & Bacon.

Rippe, J., Ross, J., Gurry, M., Hitzhusen, J., & Freedson, P. (July 1985). Cardiovascular Effects of Walking. *Proceedings of the Second International Conference of Physical Activity, Aging, and Sports,* p. 47.

Rippe, J., Ross, J., McCarron, R., Porcari, J., Kline, G., Ward, A., Gurry, M., & Freedson, P. (1986). One-Mile Walk Time Norms for Healthy Adults. *Medicine and Science in Sports and Exercise,* 18, S21.

Rippe, J. M., Ward, A., & Freedson, P. (1988). Walking for Health and Fitness. In *Encyclopedia Brittanica Medical and Health Annual.*

Robbins, G., Powers, D., & Burgess, S. (1999). *A Wellness Way of Life.* 4th ed. New York: McGraw Hill.

Rockport Company. (1999). Take the Rockport Fitness Walking Test Marlboro, MA: Rockport Walking Institute.

Rosato, F., *Jogging and Walking for Health and Fitness.* 4th ed. (2000). Belmont, CA: Wadsworth/Thomson.

Ross, J., Gurry, M., Ward, A., Walcott, G., Hitzhusen, J., & Rippe, J. (1986). Accuracy of Predicted Max Heart Rate in the Elderly. *Medicine and Science in Sports and Exercise*, 18, S95.

Schwartz, L. (1987). *Heavyhands Walking.* Emmaus, PA: Rodale.

Seiger, L. H., Kanipe, D., Vanderpool, K. & Barnes, D. (1998). *Fitness and Wellness Strategies.* 2d ed. New York: McGraw Hill.

Seiger, L. H. & Richter, J. (1997). *Your Health, Your Style: Strategies for Wellness.* New York: McGraw Hill.

Siegel, A. J. (Nov./Dec. 1988). New Insights about Obesity and Exercise. *Your Patient and Fitness in Cardiology* (Vol. 2, No. 6). McGraw-Hill, Minneapolis, MN.

Sweetgall, R., & Dignam, J. (1986). *The Walker's Journal.* Newark, DE: Creative Walking.

Sweetgall, R., Rippe, J., & Katch, F. (1985). *Rockport's Fitness Walking.* New York: Putnam.

Thaxton, N. A. (1988). *Pathways to Fitness: Foundations, Motivation, Applications.* New York: Harper & Row.

Tufts University Diet and Nutrition Letter. (June 1992). *Fifty Simple Ways to Improve Your Diet* (Vol. 10, No. 4). Park Place, NY.

Tufts University Diet and Nutrition Letter. (July 1992). *Government Gives New Shape to Eating Right* (Vol. 10, No. 5). Park Place, NY.

Turner, L. W., Sizer, F. S., Whitney, E. N., & Wilks, B. B. (1992). *Life Choices: Health Concepts and Strategies.* 2d ed. St. Paul: West.

Van Itallie, T. B., & Kral, J. G. (August 28, 1981). The Dilemma of Morbid Obesity. *Journal of the American Medical Association*, 246, 999–1003.

Vitale, F. (1973). *Individualized Fitness Programs.* Englewood Cliffs, NJ: Prentice-Hall.

Walcott, G., Coleman, R., MacVeigh, M., Ross, J., Gurry, M., Ward, A., Kline, G., & Rippe, J. (1986). Heart Rate and $\dot{V}O_2$ max Response to Weighted Walking. *Medicine and Science in Sports and Exercise*, 18, S28.

Walking for Fitness, a Round Table. (October 1986). *The Physician and Sportsmedicine*, 14(10), 145–149.

Ward, A., Wilkie, S., O'Hanley, S., Trask, C., Kallmes, D., Kleinerman, J., Crawford, B., Freedson, P., & Rippe, J. (1987). Estimation of $\dot{V}O_2$ max in Overweight Females. *Medicine and Science in Sports and Exercise*, 19, 528.

Weinberg, R., Caldwell, P., Cornelius, W., Jackson, A., & Smith, J. (1982). *Health Related Fitness: Theory and Practice.* Topeka, KS: Jostens.

Wilkie, S., O'Hanley, S., Ward, A., Zwiren, L., Freedson, P., Crawford, B., Kleinerman, J., & Rippe, J. (1987). Estimation of $\dot{V}O_2$ max from a One-Mile Walk Test Using Recovery Heart Rate. *Medicine and Science in Sports and Exercise*, 19, 528.

Yanker, G. (1983). *The Complete Book of Exercisewalking.* Chicago: Contemporary.

Yanker, G. (1985). *Gary Yanker's Walking Workouts.* New York: Warner.

Zwiren, L. D., Freedson, P. S., Ward, A., Wilkie, S., & Rippe, J. (1987). Prediction of $\dot{V}O_2$ max: Comparison of 5 Submaximal Tests. *Medicine and Science in Sports and Exercise*, 19, 564.

# INDEX

## A

"ABC's for Health" dietary guidelines, 139–140
accountability for health choices, 190
activity patterns, 4, 14, 15, 150, 157
adductor, trunk, neck, and shoulder stretch, 64–65
adherence to exercise and fitness, 165–181
adventure walking, 7
aerobic, defined, 14
aerobic exercise
    amount and frequency, 17–19
    benefits of, 14–19
    for fat loss, 158–159
    gradual adaptation, 92–93
    recovery time, 92–93
age-predicted maximum heart rate (APMHR), 85, 86, 87–89, 97
air pollution, 14, 54, 136
alcohol, 137
American body weight/fat levels, 150–151
American College of Sports Medicine, 158
American Heart Association walking program, 85, 90, 170
antioxidants, 136
anxiety and depression, benefits of walking, 25–26
APMHR (age-predicted maximum heart rate), 85, 86, 87–89, 97
appearance and aerobic exercise, 19
appetite, 127
arm swings, 9, 103–104, 117
attitude, positive, 9, 168, 191

## B

backpacks, 38
balance of healthy choices, 191
basal metabolic rate (BMR), 152
behavior
    affecting health, 197–198
    modification of, 156–157, 163–164
believing in exercise, 168
bicycling, 16

blood circulation, 17, 62
blood pressure, cold weather precautions, 46
BMR (basal metabolic rate), 152
body alignment and posture, 100, 109
body composition, 93
body suits, 37
body weight/body fatness, 149–164. *See also* Nutrition and wellness
    adherence to exercise and fitness, 165–181
    and aerobic exercise, 18
    American body weight/fat levels, 150–151
    basal metabolic rate (BMR), 152
    behavior modification, 156–157, 163–164
    benefits of healthy weight, 152–153
    changing eating behaviors, 156–157
    creeping obesity, 152
    dieting and weight loss, 153–154
    eating disorders, 152
    essential fat, 151
    fat management for life, 154–159
    gaining weight, 160
    healthy weight strategies, 154–159
    lean body weight, 151
    maintenance, 160
    motivation, 151, 154–155, 163, 165–181
    muscle *vs.* fat density, 158
    nutritional/dietary strategies, 155–156, 163
    obesity and risk factors, 151, 152–153
    percent body fat, 151
    physical activity/exercise, 157–159, 164
    recommended body weights, 150
    relapses, 159–160
    support/personal commitment, 159–160, 164
bone and aerobic exercise, 18
Brunick, Tom, 34

## C

caffeine, 137
calcium, 136–137

calorie, 127, 128–129
carbohydrates, 126, 127, 129, 130–132
cardiac rehabilitation, 23
cardiovascular endurance, 93
cardiovascular fitness, 72–73, 93
carotid artery, 73, 74
cars and walkers, 49–50
Centers for Disease Control and
    Prevention, 4
cholesterol, 133–134
clothing, 35–37, 38, 52
college/university walking classes, 5
common colds, 47
complete proteins, 130, 134
complex carbohydrates, 127, 131
connective tissue and aerobic exercise, 18
cool-down, 61, 88–89, 90
Cooper, Kenneth, 136
creeping obesity, 152

**D**

dehydration, 45, 46
depression and anxiety, benefits of
    walking, 25–26
dieting for weight loss, 153–154
disease/dysfunction and wellness, 190
dogs and walkers, 50–51
drugs, 49
duration/time of fitness walking, 87–89, 92

**E**

eating. *See* Nutrition and wellness
efficiency, 100, 101
80/20 rule in nutrition, 140–141
    endurance and aerobic exercise, 18, 93
environment, impact on wellness, 190
environmental well-being, 185, 189
essential fat, 151
estimated maximum heart rate (EMHR), 85,
    86, 87–89, 97
everyday walking, 7
exercise. *See also* Aerobic exercise; Fitness
    walking
    adapting to, 5
    advantages of, 171, 177
    amount and frequency, 14
    avoiding boredom, 170–171
    benefits of, 14, 72, 158, 171
    commitment to, 171
    contracting for, 181

convenience and enjoyment of, 168, 170
    exercise log, 171–172, 199
    forming a habit of, 169
    heart rate, 73, 75
    modifying, 173
    planning a program, 168
    prioritizing, 169, 175
    progressive adaptation, 92–93, 170
    recovery time, 92–93
    rewards for, 169–170
    social activity of, 172
    sticking with a program, 165–181

**F**

fanny packs, 38
fast foods, 141, 142
fat/fats. *See also* Body weight/body fatness
    body fat, 18
    fats as nutrients, 126, 129, 130,
        132–134
    health risks of, 155
    lipid profile, 134
    recommended amounts, 132
    reducing dietary fat, 133–134, 155–156
    types of, 132–134
fat-soluble vitamins, 130, 132, 135
feet/foot care, 54. *See also* Shoes, fitness
    walking
fiber, 127, 131–132
fitness walking, 3, 4. *See also* Exercise;
    Nutrition and wellness
    all ages, 9
    arm swings, 9, 103–104, 117
    beginners/advanced, 105, 123
    benefits of, 13–27, 27
    building fitness level, 22
    cardiac rehabilitation, 23
    cardiovascular fitness and, 9
    cars and walkers, 49–50
    clothing and equipment, 29–41, 202
    contracting for, 181
    cost of, 21
    daily routine/lifelong habit, 20, 25
    defensive walking, 50
    and dogs, 50–51
    dropout rate, 21
    duration/time, 87–89, 92
    exercise log, 171–172, 199
    fitness categories/levels, 20, 76–78, 83
    FITT, 87, 91–92, 151, 158

flexibility, 94
frequency, 87, 91
heart rate, 91
intensity, 87–89, 91, 105–107
leg movement, 9, 104, 105, 121
low-impact activity, 23
medical clearance, 44, 57, 73
mileage in a program, 88–89
modifying, 173
overtraining, 53–54
physical fitness benefits, 93–95
popularity of, 11
programs for, 85–97
progressive adaptation, 92–93, 170
psychological benefits of, 25–26
readiness for, 57
recovery, 92–93
rehabilitation of injuries, 22
safety, 2, 10, 20–21, 43–57, 74
social activity and, 22
stretching, 61–67, 69, 94, 103
techniques for, 99–123
type for aerobic exercise, 87, 92
types of, 7–9
walking speed, 123
walking surfaces, 52–53
walking tapes, 201
warm-up/cool-down, 59–69, 88–89, 90
FITT (Frequency, Intensity, Time, and
    Type), 87, 91–92, 151, 158
flexibility, 59–69, 94, 103
folic acid, 135
Food Guide Pyramid, 126, 138–141, 155
food safety, 139
free radicals, 136
frequency of fitness walking, 87–89, 91
frostbite, 46

**G**

genetics, impact on wellness, 190
gliding motion, 104, 105, 121
glucose, 127, 130–131
goals of walking program, 22, 167

**H**

habits and behaviors with food, 156–157
hamstring stretch, 65–66
hand weights, 39, 54
hats/gloves, 37
HDL (high density lipoproteins), 133–134

health, 184–185, 190–192
*Healthy People 2010*, 1, 2, 3, 149–150
heart
    and aerobic exercise, 17
    age-predicted maximum heart rate
        (APMHR), 85, 86, 87–89, 97
    angina precautions, 46
    beginner/advanced rates, 91
    Cardiovascular fitness, 72–73
    estimated maximum heart rate (EMHR),
        85, 86, 87–89, 97
    rate during exercise, 73, 75, 90
    rate monitor, 31, 38
heat-related problems, 35, 45
heel contact, 101, 111
heel cup of walking shoes, 34
heel-to-toe roll, 101–102, 113
high density lipoproteins (HDL), 133–134
hiking, 7
hill walking, 106
hip movement, 104, 119
horizontal energy, 101, 104
hot weather walking, 45
humor and laughter in lifestyle, 192
hunger, 127, 128
hyperthermia, 35
hypothermia, 45, 46

**I**

immunity/resistance to disease, 19
inactivity, 4, 157
incomplete proteins, 130, 134
injuries, 44
    heat-related problems, 45
    walking rehabilitation and, 22
inner shoe sole, 31, 32
intensity of fitness walking, 87–89, 91,
    105–107
iron, 136–137

**J**

jogging, 16

**K**

Ketchum, Brad, Jr., 34
kilocalorie, 127, 128

**L**

lacing of walking shoes, 34
LDL (low density lipoproteins), 133–134

lean body weight, 151, 160
leg glide and movement, 104, 105, 121
levels of fitness, 76–78, 83
life expectancy, 3
lifestyle, 185
    behaviors affecting health, 190,
        197–198
    causes of death, 14–15
    cumulative effect of, 189–190
    fat management strategies, 154–159
    humor and laughter, 192
    moderation, 191–192
    personalized healthy choices, 192
    positive changes, 191
    prevention, 192
    sedentary, 14, 15
    strategies for health and well-being,
        190–192
    to wellness, 189–190
lipids. *See* Fat/fats
low back stretch, 65–66
low density lipoproteins (LDL), 133–134
lunge and shoulder stretch, 63–64
lungs and aerobic exercise, 18

**M**

major minerals, 130
mall walking, 5, 6, 46, 202
medical care, impact on wellness, 190
medical clearance, 44, 57, 73
mental benefits of walking, 25
mid-sole, shoes, 31, 32
mileage in walking program, 88–89
minerals, 130, 136–137
modifying exercises, 173
monounsaturated fats, 133
motion control shoe model, 30
motivation, 151, 154–155
    for exercise and fitness, 165–181
    strategies for maintaining,
        167–173, 179
muscle
    and aerobic exercise, 18
    endurance training, 93–95
    soreness and injury, 44

**N**

National Healthy Interview Survey, 3
neck stretch, 64–65
night walking, 38, 52

noise pollution, 55
nutrition and wellness, 125–147. *See also*
    Body weight/body fatness
    assessment of food choices, 143–147
    behavior modification, 156–157
    categories of nutrients, 126–127
    changing eating behaviors, 156–157
    80/20 rule, 140–141
    fast foods, 141
    Food Guide Pyramid, 126, 138–141
    food labels, 141, 142
    food patterns, 126, 138, 156
    food safety, 139
    gaining weight, 160
    nutrition defined, 126–127
    portion size, 155
    reducing dietary fat, 155–156
    social and emotional dimension of, 128
    strategies for permanent fat
        management, 155–156
    wellness components, 129

**O**

obesity, 21, 151, 152–153, 157
optimal health, 185, 186
outer sole, shoes, 30, 32
overtraining, 45, 53–54
oxygen, 14–19

**P**

pace, 87–92, 100, 101
Parlov, Andrey, 9
pedometer, 38
percent body fat, 151
physical environment, impact on
    wellness, 190
physical well-being, 185, 188
pollution
    air, 14, 54, 136
    noise, 55
polyunsaturated fats, 133
positive attitude, 9, 168, 191
posture and alignment, 21–22, 100, 109
pregnancy and fitness walking, 23–24
prevention and wellness, 185, 192
prioritizing exercise, 169, 175
programs for fitness walking, 85–97, 168
progressive adaptation to exercise,
    92–93, 170
protein, 129, 130, 134

psychological well-being, 185, 187–188
  benefits of walking, 25–26
  impact of aerobic exercise, 19
psychosocial environment, impact on
  wellness, 190
pulse, 73, 75, 81
pulsemeter, 31, 38
push-off technique, 101, 103, 115

**Q**

quadricep and shin stretch, 65
quality of life, 3, 26

**R**

racewalking, 4, 8, 9, 31, 34, 104–105, 123
radial artery, 73, 74
reflective material, 38, 52
relapse to unhealthy habits, 151, 159–160
resistance training, 93–95, 158
rocker bottom, 101
rocker-shaped shoe sole, 30, 31, 34
Rockport Fitness Walking Program,
  85–97, 170
Rockport Fitness Walking Test, 71–83
routine daily walking, 24

**S**

safety, 50
  and fitness walking, 2, 10, 20–21,
    43–57, 74
  food handling, 139
saturated fats, 127, 132–133
sauna suits, 31, 37
scheduling time for exercise, 169
sedentary lifestyle, 14, 15, 150, 157
sedentary living. *See* Inactivity
self-esteem, benefits of walking, 26
shin and quadricep stretch, 65
shoes, fitness walking, 5–7
  flexibility, 33
  motion control, 30
  parts of, 29–35
  quality, 34
  reflective material, 38, 52
  shopping for, 30, 34–35, 41
  size and comfort, 33
shoulder stretch, 63–65
simple carbohydrates, 127, 131
skiing, 2
sleeping, benefits of walking, 26

smoking, compared to inactivity, 4
smooth walking technique, 104, 105, 121
snowshoeing, 7
social activity of exercise, 172
social well-being, 185, 188
speed, 100, 101
spiritual well-being, 185, 188
stairwalking, 9, 107
starches, 130
static stretching, 61, 62–63, 94
step aerobics, 16
strength training, 93–95, 158
stress, impact of exercise, 19, 24, 26
stretching, 61–67, 69, 94, 103
stride length, 100, 101, 119
"Striders, The," 4
strolling, 7, 8
sugars, 130, 140
sunglasses, 38
Surgeon General's Report, 1, 3–4
swimming, 2, 16

**T**

techniques for fitness walking, 99–123
tennis, 2
testing
  cardiovascular fitness, 72–73
  Rockport Fitness Walking Test, 71–83
time/duration of fitness walking,
  87–89, 92
toe box of walking shoes, 32, 34
trace minerals, 130
trans-fatty acid, 127, 133
treadmill walking, 107
trunk stretching, 64–65

**U**

underfatness, 151, 152
University of Massachusetts Medical
  School, 73, 86
unsaturated fats, 127, 133
upper shoe, 31, 32, 33
U.S. Department of Agriculture (USDA)
  dietary guidelines, 126, 138
  Food Guide Pyramid, 155
  recommended body weights, 150
U.S. Department of Health and Human
  Services
  dietary guidelines, 138, 139
  recommended body weights, 150

## V

vertical energy, 101, 104
vitamins, 130
    antioxidants, 136
    folic acid, 135
    functions of, 134–135
    supplements, 135–136
    types of, 134–136
vocational well-being, 185, 188
volksmarch, 3, 4
volksport, 3, 4

## W

"Walkers and Talkers, The," 4
walking
    classes, 5
    clubs, 4, 172–173, 202
    events, 4, 173
    shoes, 5–6
    speed, 87–92, 123
    sticks/canes, 39, 50–51
    tours, 6, 202
*Walking for a Healthy Heart*, 90
Walking-for-Fitness Exercise Log, 171, 199

*Walking* magazine, 34
warm-up, 60–61, 88–89, 90
water, 130, 137, 156
    aerobics, 16
    walking, 108
water-soluble vitamins, 130, 135
weather
    alternative environments, 107–108
    clothing for, 35–37
    extreme conditions, 44
    hot and cold, 45, 46
    walking in rain, 48–49
weight and body fatness. *See* Body
    weight/body fatness
weights and walking, 54
wellness
    defined, 184–185
    influences on, 190
    level of, 195–196
    lifestyle strategies, 190–192
    and nutrition, 125–147
    preventive measures, 192
    wheel of, 196
wellness-illness continuum, 185, 186